Mary Lou Uttermohlen

NEW ORLEANS
Classic
BRUNCHES

NEW ORLEANS *Classic* BRUNCHES

KIT WOHL

PELICAN PUBLISHING COMPANY

GRETNA 2012

The word "Pelican" and the depiction of a pelican
are trademarks of Pelican Publishing Company, Inc.,
and are registered in the
U.S. Patent and Trademark Office.

ISBN 9781589808409

Printed in China
Published by Pelican Publishing Company, Inc.
1000 Burmaster Street, Gretna, Louisiana 70053

IN MEMORY OF

Archie A. Casharian

FRIEND, GENTLEMAN, RESTAURATEUR

CONTENTS

"DON'T YOU JUST LOVE THOSE LONG RAINY AFTERNOONS IN NEW ORLEANS WHEN AN HOUR ISN'T JUST AN HOUR— BUT A LITTLE PIECE OF ETERNITY DROPPED INTO YOUR HANDS—AND WHO KNOWS WHAT TO DO WITH IT?"

—TENNESSEE WILLIAMS

Brunch. A special meal, often leisurely, occasionally decadent. A meal that's even celebrated by its own cocktails, such as the Bloody Mary or the Mimosa. Brunch is an opportunity to be a little naughty—or a lot extravagant—at the table.

It's said that the word "brunch," a combination of the words "breakfast" and "lunch," was first used in a 1895 advertisement. Some insist that Sunday brunch was patterned after the English hunt breakfast; others say it evolved as an after-church (or an instead-of-church) meal. Supposedly New York and Chicago popularized this combo-meal in the 1930s, after which it traveled to California, and then spread over the rest of the U.S. But however it began, this much is clear: Today, brunch is not just for Sunday.

Especially in New Orleans.

Brunch in New Orleans came to the forefront when Owen Brennan hatched the "Breakfast at Brennan's" concept at his eponymous restaurant on Royal Street, which he'd opened in 1946. The custom of a festive weekend meal combining breakfast and late lunch was readily adopted by New Orleanians, who were (are) always ready for another reason to eat and drink.

The Brennan family tree branched out in 1974 when Owens's sisters and brothers, Adelaide, Ella, Dottie, Dick and John Brennan acquired Commander's Palace.

During a meal in London, Dick had noticed a roving jazz trio. He telephoned his sister, Ella, and the jazz brunch was born—a new beat to a beloved tune, and now another New Orleans tradition.

Brunch menus took on a new rhythm, expanding to more than fancy eggs. Chefs took advantage of the new meal to flex their creative muscles. Certainly there are specialties, but as you will see, brunch today offers a wealth of dishes you'd like to eat at any time of day. Establishments all across the Big Easy have created their own brunches. Some are casual. Some are dress-up events. The rest are everything in-between. Almost all are wonderful.

A final note: Because the weather usually cooperates, brunch outdoors is hugely popular in New Orleans.

Once upon a time, as a green copywriter, I questioned the line, "Dine al fresco in our verdant courtyard," for a client restaurant's brunch advertisement. The crusty restaurateur read it, looked at me over his glasses. "Okay, but who the hell is Al Fresco?"

I like to think of Al Fresco as the patron spirit of a Big Easy brunch, And so, the next time you find yourself contemplating a brunch as only this town can do it, even if you're going to eat indoors, please be sure you invite Al Fresco.

–Kit Wohl

EGGS & ENTREES

Egg poaching techniques vary as much as the recipes.

The easy way is to fill a skillet or saucepan with two or three inches of water, bringing it to a simmer. Avoid broken yolks by cracking the egg into a cup or saucer before sliding the whole egg into the simmering water.

Using a spoon, baste them for just three or four minutes to cook the yolks to the preferred softness. Remove with a slotted spoon and drain. Specific poaching pans or rubber cups are available. The eggs are prettier. The taste is the same.

The sous vide technique requires equipment and time. A large number of perfectly poached, shaped eggs result, still in the shell. The eggs can be ignored while they loll about in a controlled warm water spa. The whites have an almost translucent look, but are exquisitely cooked. The taste is superb.

For a small group, simply poach the eggs just before use. For a large group, expedite the process by poaching the eggs a day ahead. To pre-poach 12 eggs, bring 2 quarts of water to a simmer in a large saucepan and add 4 tablespoons of white vinegar.

Fill a large bowl with ice and water and place at the side of the stove. Working fast, crack an egg into a small bowl or saucer, then quickly slip it into the simmering water just above the water's surface and repeat. Try to keep track of the timing so the earlier ones do not overcook. Adding the eggs in saucers two at a time helps. Poach for three to four minutes, until the whites are just firm and the yolks are still quite soft to the touch.

Using a slotted spoon, gently retrieve the eggs in the order they were placed in the pan and lower them into the iced water. Repeat with the remaining eggs, two at a time. Leave the eggs in the ice bath until they are all poached. Gently retrieve the eggs and trim off any ragged edges with kitchen shears, returning them to the cold water. Cover the bowl securely and refrigerate for up to 24 hours. Place the cold poached eggs in simmering water for 30 seconds to reheat before serving.

Chef Leah Chase told me that soft-boiled eggs can be used to replace poached, if time or technique is a consideration. She is an exceptionally smart lady.

MISS ANNIE'S BLUEBERRY MUFFINS

MAKES 10 to 12

1 1/2 cups	all-purpose flour
3/4 cup	white granulated sugar
1/2 teaspoon	salt
2 teaspoons	baking powder
1/3 cup	vegetable oil
1 egg	beaten
1/3 cup	milk
1/2 teaspoon	vanilla
1 cup	fresh blueberries, if frozen, keep frozen and drain

Preheat oven to 400°F.

Grease muffin cups or use muffin liners. Using a medium sized bowl, combine flour, 3/4 cup sugar, salt and baking powder. In a separate mixing bowl, combine the vegetable oil, egg, vanilla and milk. Stir egg mixture into the flour mixture; mix thoroughly. Carefully fold in blueberries. Fill muffin cups to the top, and place in oven.

Bake for 20 to 25 minutes in the preheated oven, until done when a toothpick is inserted and comes out clean, or press top lightly with finger and it springs back. The medium or small size muffins will require less baking time, so adjust and check accordingly.

THE PONTCHARTRAIN
EGGS & CORNED BEEF HASH

The hotel's corned beef hash recipe required much research until we discovered the secret from a former colleague. How did it get so nice and crisp, we wanted to know. How did the flavor come through so elegantly? It was made from Hormel brand Mary Kitchen corned beef hash was the surprising answer. We suspect that Annie Laurie, the breakfast cook and baker was busy and saved delicious time with her shortcut. If you'd like to recreate a feast, also stir up her blueberry biscuit recipe, to the left.

SERVES 4

1 tablespoon	olive oil	4	eggs, poached or over easy
1 15-ounce can	Hormel Mary Kitchen brand corned beef hash		

Coat with olive oil and heat a griddle or large frying pan to almost smoking hot. The oil will have little ripples running across the top. While the oil Is heating, divide corned beef hash evenly to make 4 large patties, each about 3/4 inch thick, and press down using a spatula, heating throughout while creating a nice crisp exterior. Turn and crisp the other side.

Meanwhile, poach the eggs in a skillet or medium sized pan by bringing 1 inch to 2 inches of water to a simmer. Crack each egg into a saucer first in case the yolk breaks. Slide the egg into the water, continuing to simmer until the whites are set and the yolk is done to medium soft, about 2 to 3 minutes.

Place a corned beef patty on each plate. Remove the eggs from the water using a slotted spoon.

Tip: Finely chop and saute an onion to mix into the corned beef hash before heating it. A splash of Louisiana hot sauce such as Crystal or Tabasco gives it a little Big Easy kick.

CHEF MICHELLE MCRANEY, MR. B'S BISTRO
Eggs & Crab Meat Hash

In the Brennan family tradition, Mr. B's Bistro makes brunch a weekly event. Chef Michelle McRaney works closely with Cindy Brennan to salute the classic dishes and create new ones.

SERVES 4

3 tablespoons	vegetable oil
3	russet potatoes, peeled and in 1/2-inch dice
2 tablespoons	unsalted butter
1/2	medium onion, diced
1/2	medium red bell pepper, diced
1/2	medium yellow bell pepper, diced
1	garlic clove, minced

1 pound	jumbo lump crab meat, picked over
3 tablespoons	fresh chives, minced
	Kosher salt and freshly ground black pepper to taste
1 teaspoon	distilled white vinegar
8	large eggs
1 cup	orange hollandaise sauce *(page 93)*

In a large nonstick skillet heat oil over high heat until hot but not smoking. Add potatoes and sauté, stirring constantly, until golden brown, about 10 minutes.

In another large skillet melt 2 tablespoons butter over moderate heat. Add onion, bell peppers, and garlic and cook 3 minutes, or until just wilted. Add potatoes, crab meat, chives, and salt and pepper and keep warm.

Butter bottom of a 2-quart heavy saucepan and add 1 1/4 inches water. Add vinegar and bring to a simmer. Break 1 egg into a cup and slide into water. Repeat with remaining 3 eggs, spacing them apart, and poach at a bare simmer until whites are firm but yolks are still runny, 2 to 3 minutes. Transfer eggs as cooked with a slotted spoon to paper towels to drain and season with salt and pepper. Serve hash topped with poached eggs and hollandaise sauce.

Proprietor Cindy Brennan's friends who insist on her Bloody Marys for Mardi Gras parades. Anytime is a good time.

BLOODY MARY
MAKES 1 drink

1 1/2 ounces	vodka
1/3 cup	tomato juice
1/4 teaspoon	Worcestershire sauce
1/4 teaspoon	beef broth
1/4 teaspoon	horseradish
splash	Rose's lime juice
3 dashes	Tabasco
1 dash	freshly ground black pepper
1 dash	celery salt
	lime wedge, celery stick and two pickled green beans for garnish

Fill a tall glass two-thirds full with ice cubes. Add all ingredients. Cover and shake vigorously. Garnish with lime, celery, and green beans.

VIRGIN MARY

Simply exclude the alcohol and follow the recipe above.

CHEF TOMMY DIGIOVANNI, ARNAUD'S
EGGS BENEDICT

Arnaud's Brunch and Jazz is an every Sunday event. Founded in 1918, the restaurant has always been family owned and operated. Exquisitely restored by the late Archie A. Casbarian, the grande dame's legacy continues with brother and sister Archie and Katy Casbarian as co-proprietors. Their elegant mother, Jane Casbarian, keeps everything in good taste.

SERVES 6

12	poached eggs *(page 11)*		1 1/2 cups	freshly-made hollandaise sauce *(page 93)*
6	English muffins			Dash of paprika
12 slices	Canadian bacon			Sprigs of fresh curly parsley, for garnish

Warm 6 dinner plates in a low oven and poach the eggs (or warm 12 pre-poached eggs). Place 2 toasted muffin halves on each plate, cut side up, and top each one with a slice of warmed Canadian bacon. Place a poached egg on top of the bacon and ladle about 1/4 cup of hollandaise sauce over each. Sprinkle with a little paprika for color and garnish each plate with a sprig or two of curly parsley. Serve immediately.

While Eggs Benedict does not call for creamed spinach, by adding it to the recipe, it becomes what is commonly recognized as Eggs Sardou, a different recipe than the one in this book created by Antoine's Restaurant.

FRENCH 75
MAKES 1 cocktail

The French 75 has always been so popular at Arnaud's that the bar is named in honor of the cocktail. It would be difficult to imagine a happier combination than fine champagne and excellent cognac.

1 1/2 ounces	cognac
1 teaspoon	fresh lemon juice
1/4 teaspoon	simple syrup *(page 23)*
4 ounces	Champagne
	Twist of lemon

Place the cognac, lemon juice and simple syrup in a shaker filled with ice and shake only long enough to chill. Pour into a frosted champagne glass, top with champagne and add a lemon twist. Serve immediately.

CHEF LAZONE RANDOLPH, BRENNAN'S
Eggs Hussarde

Brennan's legendary chef Paul Blangé, who also created Bananas Foster, modified Eggs Benedict to suit his tastes. The Canadian bacon is placed on Holland Rusks, then poached eggs layered between both Hollandaise and Marchand de Vin sauces. It is served accompanied by a broiled tomato.

SERVES 4

8	Holland Rusks (available in most grocery stores)		8	poached eggs *(page 11)*
2 cups	Marchand de Vin sauce *(recipe below)*		2 tablespoons	unsalted butter
2 cups	Hollandaise sauce *(page 93)*		8	slices Canadian bacon (or ham)

Prepare the Marchand de Vin sauce and the Hollandaise sauce. Keep warm. Poach the eggs and keep warm. Melt butter in a large sauté pan and warm the Canadian bacon over low heat. Place 2 Holland Rusks on each plate and cover with slices of warm Canadian bacon. Spoon the Marchand de Vin sauce over the meat, then set a poached egg on each slice. Ladle Hollandaise sauce over the eggs and serve.

MARCHAND DE VIN SAUCE

6 tablespoons	butter		2 tablespoons	Worcestershire sauce
1/2 cup	onion, finely chopped		2 cups	beef stock
1 1/2 teaspoon	garlic, finely chopped		1/2 cup	red wine
1/2 cup	scallions, finely chopped		11/2 teaspoons	thyme leaves
1/2 cup	boiled ham, finely chopped		1	bay leaf
1/2 cup	mushrooms, finely chopped		1/2 cup	fresh parsley, finely chopped
1/3 cup	all-purpose flour			Salt and black pepper

Using a large saucepan or Dutch oven over medium high heat, melt the butter and sauté the onion, garlic, scallions and ham for 5 minutes. Add the mushrooms, reduce the heat to medium and cook for 2 minutes. Blend in the flour and cook, stirring for 4 minutes, then add the Worcestershire sauce, beef stock, wine, thyme and bay leaf. Simmer until the sauce thickens, about 1 hour.

Before serving, remove the bay leaf and add the parsley. Season with salt and pepper.

ABSINTHE SUISSESSE

Founder Owen Brennan made breakfast a wakeup call for New Orleans. The restaurant continues to be a family operation and one of the city's legendary great establishments. The old Creole home and patio are fine examples of classic French Quarter architecture.

SERVES 4

1/2 cup	Herbsaint (Absinthe, Ricard or Pernod may be substituted)
1 large	egg white
1/4 cup	half-and-half
1/4 cup	simple syrup *(page 23)*
1 cup	crushed ice

Put all the drink ingredients in a blender at high speed for 30 seconds.

Serve in chilled old fashioned or wine glasses.

"Dook," Edgar Chase IV, Leah and Dooky Chase's grandson, is now chef alongside Leah. "He graduated from Le Cordon Bleu in Paris," she says. "Now he's cooking at Le Cordon Noir in New Orleans."

A tiny sandwich shop was transformed into one of the country's most culturally significant restaurants through sheer hard work and necessity. Dooky Chase's became a political hub and haven in the 60s during the Civil Rights movement, and no one ever left hungry; Leah Chase made certain of it then, and still does. However, she did insist that the freedom riders shower (at a friend's place around the corner) before entering the restaurant, properly clean.

Today, race, creed or zip code do not matter a whit at Dooky Chase's restaurant but guests are still expected to be tidy.

CHEF DOOK CHASE, DOOKY CHASE'S

EGGS NEW ORLEANS

Many brunch dishes are creative versions of favorites, given a personal twist by thoughtful chefs. As an original Chef Dook's grandmother Chef Leah Chase, is not only a master, but also an inventive one. Dook inherited her creativity and practicality, making this recipe his own

Eggs New Orleans is simple, and simply a delicious combination. Poached, or during busy times soft boiled eggs are placed atop a generous serving of Crab Meat Imperial.

SERVES 6

CRAB MEAT IMPERIAL

1 pound	fresh, jumbo, lump crab meat	1/4 cup	green onions, minced
1/2 cup	green bell pepper, diced	1 cup	Béchamel sauce
1/4 cup	red bell pepper diced or substitute pimento	to taste	Salt, white pepper, cayenne

Preheat oven to 350°F.

Using your fingers, gently pick through the crab meat without breaking any lumps to remove any tiny bits of shell. In a medium sized oven-proof baking dish, combine all of the ingredients, except the crab meat. Lightly stir in the crab meat so lumps are not broken.

Bake in 350°F oven for 15 minutes.

Poach two eggs per person, or, if in pinch, soft boil them.

Place a scoop of Crab Meat Imperial on each plate beside the eggs and serve.

BÉCHAMEL OR SAUCE BLANCHE (WHITE SAUCE)

White sauce is one of the five French mother sauces, the basis for innumerable variations of flavorings and use.

2 tablespoons	butter	1 cup	hot milk
2 tablespoons	all purpose flour (or cornstarch)	1/4 teaspoon	salt
		1/4 teaspoon	white pepper

In a heavy bottomed skillet, melt butter over a medium heat but do not let it brown. Blend in flour and stir continuously, making a smooth paste, while cooking 6 to 7 minutes. Slowly add warmed milk, season with salt and pepper continuing to stir while bringing it to a boil and the sauce thickens. Lower the heat and cook, stirring another 2 to 3 minutes.

Eggs & Red Bean Cakes

Ralph Brennan is another of this generation's Brennan cousins who has made a significant impact on the hospitality scene. In addition to the old casino building next door to City Park, he created the popular Redfish Grill in the French Quarter, Heritage Grill, Café b, Café NOMA and Jazz Kitchen.

SERVES 12

RED BEAN CAKE

1 pound	dried red beans	2 cups	flour
1	jalapeno pepper, seeded and chopped	2 cups	bread crumbs
		2 cups	egg wash (lightly beaten egg)
1	onion, chopped		Salt and pepper
1 quart	chicken stock		Oil for frying

Soak the red beans overnight in water and drain. Sauté the onions and jalapeno, add the soaked, red beans and cover with chicken stock. Allow to simmer on medium heat until the beans are soft. Season to taste with salt and pepper. Puree the mixture, and then allow to cool.

Scoop the bean mixture into 24 patties of 1/4 cup each. Bread each patty by dredging in the flour, egg wash then bread crumbs, then line up and set aside on a sheet pan. In a heavy-bottomed skillet, heat the oil until a drop of water spatters. Using tongs, fry each patty on both sides in the hot oil.

SWEET ONION ANDOUILLE SAUSAGE GRAVY

MAKES 1 QUART

1/2 cup	unsalted butter		Pinch of sugar
5	sweet onions, julienned	1 1/2 quarts	veal stock
1 1/4 pounds	andouille sausage, minced	1/2 quart	heavy cream
	Salt and pepper		

In a large pot over medium heat, melt the butter. Add the onions and sauté until translucent. Add the andouille sausage and continue to simmer over medium heat. Season with a pinch of sugar and salt and pepper to taste, this will help bring out the flavors. Stir occasionally and continue to cook until it reaches a caramel color. Add veal stock and allow to reduce by 1/2. Add heavy cream and simmer for 15 minutes. Adjust the salt and pepper.

POACHED EGGS

24 eggs   poached *(page 11)*

To serve, place 2 red bean cakes on each plate. Top each with a poached egg and ladle the Andouille gravy over them. Garnish and with serve with any extra gravy on the side.

MINT JULEP

SERVES 12

1 cup	muddled fresh mint leaves
3 cups*	bourbon
3 cups	simple syrup
12 sprigs	fresh mint leaves for garnish

Reserving 12 mint leafs for garnish, remove the leaves from stems and muddle (crush) the remaining mint leaves. Fill 12 glasses with crushed ice and divide the muddled mint between them. Add 2-ounces of bourbon and 2-ounces of simple syrup to each glass. Top with mint sprig.

SIMPLE SYRUP

2 cups	water
2 cups	granulated sugar

In a small saucepan combine water and sugar and bring to a boil over high heat until the sugar is completely dissolved. Allow syrup to cool, approximately 1 hour. It may be stored in a covered container in the refrigerator.

*NOTE: More bourbon may be used if desired.

Antoine's is America's oldest family-run restaurant, started by young Antoine Alciatore. Rick Blount, the fifth-generation chief executive officer, uses the same front door as Antoine did in 1840.

Second generation Jules Alciatore created Café Brûlot Diabolique (devilishly burned coffee) in the 1890s. The flaming concoction of coffee, brandy, and spices became a sleight of hand to disguise alcohol during Prohibition.

Almost every guest is familiar with the jolly devil, or jester, as you choose to believe, who holds the brûlot bowl aloft. It is a traditional finale for a grand meal.

CHEF MICHAEL REGUA, ANTOINE'S

Eggs Sardou

An extravagant celebration dish, Eggs Sardou highlights artichoke bottoms, anchovies and hollandaise sauce. It was created at Antoine's and named after 19th century French playwright Victorien Sardou, in honor of his visit to New Orleans. A special Antoine's touch is fresh asparagus, lightly battered and fried then served crisscrossed on the plate.

SERVES: 6

12	freshly-cooked artichoke bottoms or two 13.5 ounce cans, drained and rinsed	1 1/2 cups	freshly-made hollandaise sauce *(page 93)*
1 tablespoon	unsalted butter (optional, only if using canned artichoke bottoms)	for garnish	dash of paprika
		for garnish	parsley, chopped
12	anchovies split in half lengthwise	for garnish	red bell pepper, chopped
12	eggs or pre-poached eggs *(page 11)*		

If using canned artichoke bottoms, melt the butter in a small sauve pan over medium heat. Add the artichoke bottoms and cook gently, turning over once, for about 2 minutes, just to heat through without browning. Remove the pan from the heat, cover, and set aside in a warm place. Warm the dinner plates in a low oven and poach the eggs. Place 2 artichoke bottoms on each plate, well side up, and crisscross 2 anchovy halves in artichoke bottom. Place a poached egg on top. Ladle about 1/4 cup of Hollandaise Sauce over the top of each egg, garnish and serve.

Café Brûlot

SERVES: 6

2	cinnamon sticks	4	sugar cubes
6	whole cloves	1/2 cup	brandy
1/4 cup	grated lemon or	3 cups	hot, strong black coffee
1	orange peel, curled in thin spiral or	1	long, fireplace match
1/4 cup	slivered orange peel		

In a copper Brûlot bowl or chafing dish, combine the cinnamon, cloves, citrus peel and sugar cubes. Place over medium heat and crush together, using the back of a large ladle. For safety*, add the brandy to the ladle, light with a long match, then pour the flaming liqueur into the pan. Never flame the brandy in the pan. Stir thoroughly and, simmer, stirring to dissolve the sugar. As the flames begin to die out, gradually add the black coffee. Ladle into Brûlot or demitasse cups, leaving the spices and citrus peels behind.

*Flambé cooking requires diligence, awareness, safety and caution. Never flame the liqueur in the bowl, always use a ladle. It is best to perform the ceremony on a side cart, away from the guests, intake vents and draperies. After all, you are playing with fire.

CHEF ALEX HARRELL, SYLVAIN
EGGS, BISCUITS & SAUSAGE GRAVY

Sylvain is one of the French Quarter's almost secret restaurants. Walking toward Jackson Square, it is tucked into a three-story carriage house built in 1796. It is named after Jean-Francois-Marmontel and Andre Getry's one-act comic opera Sylvain, performed in New Orleans the same year. Hidden behind the restaurant is an oasis, a lush courtyard, and perfect for shady afternoons under the trees.

SERVES 6 to 8

POACHED EGGS

2 eggs, poached per person *(page 11)*

CREAM BISCUITS

2 cups	all-purpose flour	2 teaspoons	granulated sugar
1 teaspoon	salt	1 cup	heavy cream
1 tablespoon	baking powder	2 tablespoons	melted butter

SAUSAGE MILK GRAVY
MAKES 2 1/2 cups

2 tablespoons	butter	2 cups	milk
2 cups	fresh ground sausage	1 teaspoon	fresh ground pepper
2 tablespoons	all purpose flour		salt and pepper to taste
1 cup	heavy cream		Chives for garnish

TO MAKE THE BISCUITS

Preheat oven to 400°F.

Sift the dry ingredients together and fold in the heavy cream until it makes a soft dough. Turn the dough out onto a lightly floured surface, and knead to bring together. Roll out to a thickness of 1/2 of an inch, and cut with a round cutter. Place on a baking sheet and brush the tops with melted butter. Bake at 400°F for 15-18 minutes.

TO MAKE THE GRAVY

Heat the butter over medium to high heat and brown the sausage. Whisk in the flour and cook, stirring, for 5 minutes. Add the cream and milk and whisk until smooth. Reduce the heat and slowly simmer the gravy for 20 minutes. Season with salt and pepper.

To serve, place 2 biscuits on each plate. Top each with a poached egg and ladle the gravy over them. Garnish with chives and serve any extra gravy on the side.

PIMM'S CUP
MAKES 1 drink

As Antoine's restaurant opened here in 1840, Pimm's was created in England. Their Pimm's mix claims to be the original–a closely held recipe. At the 200-year old Napoleon House classical music, including Eroiqua which Beethoven composed for Napoleon, enhances the old world ambiance. New Orleans creative community make a Pimm's Cup a summertime refresher.

Around the corner at Sylvain, instead of the Pimm's Mix, they make their own concoction by muddling fresh citrus: orange, lemon and lime, poured over ice and topped with either ginger ale or lemonade.

It can be a satisfying non-alcoholic beverage.

The easy way:

Napoleon House	
1 1/4 ounces	Pimm's #1
3 ounces	lemonade
Splash	7UP
Garnish	slice of cucumber

Fill a tall 12-ounce glass with ice and add Pimm's and lemonade. Then top off the glass with 7UP.

Garnish with cucumber.

Billy has been a red bean aficionado since grammar school. His first red bean omelet was at the Coffee Pot in the French Quarter and he's been tinkering with the recipe ever since. There's no better way to use leftover red beans unless it would be for Billy's red bean soup recipe published in New Orleans Classic Gumbo and Soups. That tickled the Gourmet magazine editor's imagination and was embraced as a coveted Cookbook of the Month. He's been considering a red bean po boy with Andouille or hot sausage and gravy.

BILLY WOHL

RED BEAN OMELET

The use of a blender (or an immersion blender) forces air into the eggs by whipping, resulting in a light, fluffy omelet.

SERVES 6

1 pound	Andouille or smoked sausage (optional)	2 cups	grated cheddar cheese
10	eggs	1/2 cup	finely chopped green onion
2 cups	red beans, cooked or		Salt and pepper to taste
16 ounce	can of Blue Runner brand red beans		

In a 12-inch skillet brown and heat the sausage, remove from skillet, slice into diagonal pieces and return to the skillet. Cover to keep warm.

Whip the eggs until foamy and pale yellow. Add salt and pepper to taste. With a stove top griddle or large, heavy-bottomed skillet, heat to medium temperature and coat with clarified butter. When a drop of water hisses in the oil, it is ready. Pour in the eggs. Allow the eggs to set for about 1 minute.

Using a heat-resistant rubber spatula, carefully push the edge of the eggs into the center of the pan, while tilting the pan to allow uncooked egg to run underneath. Avoid browning by lowering the heat or moving the pan off the flame briefly to cool. Repeat until all of the egg mixture is cooked. If you prefer a well-cooked egg, flip the eggs and cook for another 30 seconds.

In a small saucepan over medium heat, warm the red beans.

Reserving a 1/2 cup each of the red beans and the cheese for garnish, add the red beans to the almost cooked eggs and then the cheese. Using a spatula, fold over into a half moon. Garnish by topping the omelet with the remaining red beans, cheese, and chopped green onions.

NOTE: To make a fluffy omelet at home that does not brown and cooks all the way through, use a low flame and cover the pan briefly to set the eggs, add the ingredients, return the lid until the cheese has melted, and using a spatula, flip over into a half moon.

CHEF MICHAEL RUOSS, CAMELLIA GRILL
CHILI-CHEESE OMELET

The use of a blender (or a hand immersion blender), rather than beating the eggs with a fork, forces air into the eggs by whipping, resulting in a light, fluffy omelet. Lower the heat immediately if the eggs begin to brown.

SERVES 1

1 teaspoon	clarified butter		3 slices	American cheese
3	eggs			Salt and fresh ground pepper
1/4 cup	chili (Hormel brand beef and bean chili is recommended.)			to taste

Using a blender, whip the eggs until foamy and pale yellow. Add salt and pepper to taste. With a stove top griddle or 9-inch, heavy-bottomed skillet, heat to medium temperature and coat with clarified butter. When a drop of water hisses in the oil, it is ready. Pour in the eggs. Allow the eggs to set for about one minute.

Using a heat-resistant rubber spatula, carefully push the edge of the eggs into the center of the pan, while tilting the pan to allow uncooked egg to run underneath. Avoid browning by lowering the heat or moving the pan off the flame briefly to cool. Repeat until all of the egg mixture is cooked. If you prefer a well-cooked egg, flip the eggs and cook for another 30 seconds.

In a small saucepan over medium heat, warm the chili.

Reserving a tablespoon each of the chili and the cheese for garnish, add the chili to the almost cooked eggs and then the cheese. Using a spatula, fold over into a half moon. Garnish by topping the omelet with the remaining chili and cheese. Add parsley or chopped green onions, if desired.

NOTE: This is not done at Camellia Grill, but for a fluffy omelet at home that does not brown and cooks all the way through, cover it briefly with a lid to set eggs, add the ingredients, return the lid until the cheese has melted. Remove the lid, and using a spatula, flip over into a half moon. Some may shout heretic, but it's easy and it works.

The oak tree out front is a New Orleans welcome. Camellia Grill is a time-honored custom for generations of New Orleanians, students from nearby universities, and visitors wearing blue jeans to black tie. It's a must-stop on the St. Charles Avenue streetcar line #43 at River Bend. The line outside is no concern–the wait is short, the friends are new. Service inside is brisk. Stools spin as stools should, starched linen napkins are folded, and straws served with a flourish underscore the old-fashioned diner.

FREEZE
MAKES 1 freeze

Along with omelets, hamburgers, and pecan pie, Camellia Grill is famous for freezes in chocolate, vanilla, orange, and coffee flavors. They're simple to whip up in a blender.

1 1/2 cups	milk
1 scoop	ice cream, chocolate, vanilla, coffee, or orange sherbet
1 teaspoon	chocolate, vanilla, or coffee extract
1 teaspoon	simple syrup *(page 23)*

Place all ingredients in a blender and pulse until foamy. Pour into a cold glass, and serve with a straw and spoon.

PETER'S PLANTERS PUNCH

A refreshing entry, this original placed in the national Tales of the Cocktail drink competition.

SERVES 1

1 1/2 ounces	Old New Orleans 3 year rum
1/2 ounce	cardamom syrup*
3 dashes	Fee Brothers Orgeat syrup
1/4 ounce	Navan vanilla liqueur
1 ounce	fresh orange juice
1 ounce	fresh lemon juice

In a stemmed water glass filled with ice build the rum, cardamom syrup, orgeat and juices, and stir. Float Navan Vanilla on top and garnish with an orange slice rolled in cayenne and sugar.

*CARDAMOM SYRUP

In a medium size sauce pan, combine a half cup water, 1 cup sugar and one tablespoon cardamom seeds. Bring to a rolling boil. Allow to cool and strain.

OYSTERS POACHED IN CREAM

Dickie Brennan has made an important mark on the restaurant scene, successfully creating three signature restaurants. Palace Cafe, Dickie Brennan's Steak House, and Bourbon House each bear his name and creativity. He was schooled as a restaurateur by Dick Brennan, his father, and Ella Brennan, his aunt, at Commander's Palace. Active in community and hospitality associations, his commitments include the James Beard Foundation's board of directors, a high honor.

SERVES 4

OYSTERS POACHED IN CREAM

4 (2-inch) slices	French bread, bias cut	1 tablespoon	fresh rosemary, minced
1 tablespoon	unsalted butter, softened	1 tablespoon	shallots, minced
for seasoning	salt and pepper	2 dozen	fresh shucked oysters
4 tablespoons	bread crumbs	4 sprigs	fresh rosemary
2 tablespoons	freshly grated Parmesan cheese	1 tablespoon	parsley, finely chopped for garnish
1 quart	heavy cream	to taste	salt and white pepper

Preheat the oven to 350°F.

Butter both sides of the French bread slices and season with salt and pepper. Place the slices on a baking sheet and toast in the oven until crisp.

In a small bowl, mix the bread crumbs and the Parmesan cheese and set aside.

In a heavy sauce pot, over medium-high heat, reduce the cream by half. Stir in the rosemary and shallots and continue to cook until it thickens a bit. Strain the sauce to remove the shallots and rosemary.

Ladle the cream into an oven-safe skillet and bring to a boil. Add the oysters and season to taste with salt and white pepper. Be careful not to over-salt the dish! Remember, the oysters are somewhat salty, as is the Parmesan cheese.

Cook for 1 to 2 minutes, or until the ends of the oysters start to curl, then remove from heat.

Sprinkle the bread crumbs and Parmesan cheese over the oysters. Broil in a 350° oven until the bread crumbs are toasted and golden brown.

To serve, place a French bread crouton in the center of each serving plate. Spoon the oysters and sauce around each crouton. Spear a rosemary sprig through each crouton and sprinkle the dish with parsley.

TRICKS OF THE TRADE: In the restaurant we serve this signature dish in individual 4-ounce French pans. For this pan roast presentation without all of the pans, serve your Oyster Pan Roast family style from a cast iron skillet

CHEF MATT REGAN, JOHN BESH'S LÜKE
FRIED CHICKEN & WAFFLES

The cast iron pan retains heat well, however it's important not to add but one piece of chicken to the pan every couple of minutes. The first piece will brown a good bit faster so add larger pieces first and likewise follow suit finishing with the smaller ones in the pan before the lid goes on.

SERVES 6
(double the amount of ingredients if 2 waffles per serving are desired)

TO FRY THE CHICKEN

1	whole chicken, cut into 8 pieces	2 tablespoons	onion powder
	Salt	2 tablespoons	garlic powder
	Freshly ground pepper	1 quart	milk
3 cups	flour		Canola oil

Salt and pepper the chicken pieces generously. Mix the flour, onion and garlic powder together. Dip the chicken in the milk and then dredge through the flour mixture to coat well.

Heat 2 inches of canola oil in a skillet to 350°F. Drop the chicken, in small batches, into the oil. Fry, covered, for 10 to 12 minutes and turn over, cooking for an additional 8 minutes. Place on paper towels to drain and season with salt and pepper immediately.

TO MAKE THE WAFFLES

1 tablespoon	sugar	1 1/2 cups	milk
2 cups	sifted flour	2	egg yolks, beaten
4 teaspoons	baking powder	6 tablespoons	melted butter
1/2 teaspoon	salt	2	egg whites, stiffly beaten

Sift together sugar, flour, baking powder and salt. Add milk to yolks and stir quickly into sifted dry ingredients. Add butter. Fold in whites. Bake in preheated waffle iron.

GRAVY

2 tablespoons	unsalted butter	2 cups	chicken stock
1	shallot, minced	6 ounces	slab or thick bacon, cut into match sticks
2	cloves garlic, minced		Salt and pepper to taste
2 tablespoons	all purpose flour		Sage leaves for garnish
2	cups milk		Chives, chopped for garnish

In a heavy bottomed skillet, melt butter over a medium heat but do not let it brown. Add the minced shallot and garlic then stir until translucent, about 2 to 3 minutes. Blend in flour and stir continuously, making a smooth paste, while cooking 6 to 7 minutes. In a separate saucepan, combine the milk with the chicken stock and warm. Slowly add warmed liquid to the flour, continuing to stir while bringing it to a boil and the gravy thickens. Lower the heat and cook, stirring another 2 to 3 minutes. Fold the crisp bacon matchsticks into the gravy.

(recipe continued at right)

(recipe continued from left)
TO MAKE THE BACON

Cut the slab or thick bacon into matchstick-sized pieces. Using a separate skillet, fry the bacon until crisp. Remove from pan with a slotted spoon or spatula, drain and fold into gravy.

TO MAKE THE SAUTÉ OF MUSHROOMS (optional)

2 tablespoons	olive oil
1	shallot, minced
1 clove	garlic, minced
1 pint	shitake mushrooms (or mushrooms of your choice), sliced
1/2 tablespoon	fresh thyme, chopped
	Salt and pepper

Using a small skillet over medium heat add the olive oil. When hot, add minced shallot and garlic then stir until translucent. Add the mushroom slices and stir until soft, about two to three minutes. Stir in the chopped thyme, then salt and pepper to taste.

Serve by placing the chicken on each plate with 1 or 2 waffles as desired. Ladle gravy over the chicken and waffles, garnish each with a sprig of thyme, sautéed mushrooms, sage leaves and sprinkle with chives.

ABITA ROOT BEER FLOAT

We used to call it a brown cow. At her restaurant Mondo in Lakeview, Chef Susan Spicer has upscaled it for the Big Easy. Cheers.

SERVES 1

1 to 2 scoops	best vanilla ice cream
12-ounce bottle	Abita Root Beer, chilled

Using a large, chilled glass, add the ice cream first. Pour the root beer over the ice cream. Serve with a long ice tea spoon, a straw, and the remaining root beer in the bottle so any extra may be used to keep topping off the drink.

(recipe continued from right)
until the butter and Crisco are in quarter size pieces. Add buttermilk and knead gently until dough comes together. Wrap in plastic and let rest in refrigerator for 15 min. Roll out dough to 1/2-inches thick and cut 1/2-inch x 1/2-inch squares. Place on a greased baking sheet, put in the oven, and bake, watching carefully, until golden brown for about 10 minutes.

To serve, place stew in a bowl and top with a half roasted or quartered chicken. Cut the biscuits and place on top.

*bouquet garni on page 91

*bouquet garni on page 91

CHEF CINDY CROSBIE, SUSAN SPICER'S MONDO
SMOTHERED CHICKEN & BISCUITS

Chef Susan Spicer had a comfortable neighborhood place in the back of her mind for years as a companion for Bayona, her famous French Quarter restaurant. With Mondo, she's realized yet another dream.

SERVES 4 to 6

ROASTED CHICKEN

2	whole chickens	1	lemon, halved
	kosher salt	1	onion, rough chopped
	rosemary springs		

STEW

1	leek diced	1	pound unsalted butter
1	yellow onion, diced	1/2 cup	all purpose flour
1	stalk celery, diced		bouquet garni* of tarragon,
1	large turnip, diced		thyme and bay leaf
1	large carrot, diced	1/2 gallon	chicken stock

4 TO 6 SMALL BISCUITS

2 cups	all purpose flour	1/4 cup	butter
3/4 tablespoon	baking powder	1/4 cup	Crisco
1/2 tablespoon	sugar	3/4 cup	buttermilk
3/4 tablespoon	salt		

HOW TO ROAST CHICKEN

Preheat oven to 375°F.

Using whole 2-1/2 pound fryers, clean and trim excess fat and skin. Remove any packaged chicken parts from the cavity and reserve to make chicken stock at another time.

Rub the chicken with kosher salt. Stuff the interior of the cavity with rosemary sprigs, onion, and halved lemon, if desired. Tie the drumsticks together over the cavity and place breast side up in a roasting pan. Put in the preheated oven and roast for about 45 minutes to 1 hour based on the size of the poultry. Remove and allow to stand for about 10 minutes so the juices settle back into the bird before carving.

HOW TO MAKE THE STEW

Sweat the vegetables in butter until onions become translucent. Add flour and make a blonde roux, cooking on low for about 8 minutes. Add chicken stock slowly, while stirring. Add bouquet garni and cook for 20 minutes on low simmer.

HOW TO MAKE THE BISCUITS

Preheat oven to 375°F.

In a large mixing bowl, combine dry ingredients with Crisco and butter. Cut together with fingers
(recipe continued at left)

ALIX & PAUL RICO
SPANISH TORTILLA

When he ran away from home as a teenager, Paul smuggled out this recipe in his country's time-honored Basque tradition. A chance meeting in Paris with a visiting restaurateur, the late Jimmy Brennan, lured Paul to New Orleans. Once here, like so many he stayed, smitten with the food, European flavors of the city and a beautiful woman. He charmed the city's artistic community, and courted Alix, preparing his tortilla for their first date. Adept at telling a good story in pictures and words, Paul prospered as the South's most talented photographer and raconteur.

With Alix, who become his wife, they are authorities and collectors of art and French antiques. An acclaimed and exacting designer, Alix notes that this is a Spanish recipe. A toast to New Orleans' Spanish and French heritage, and to their marriage, it is served to the Rico's favored guests.

SERVES 4

1 1/2 medium	russet potatoes	1/2 cup	olive oil
1 1/2 medium	yellow onions, chopped	5 large	eggs, beaten
6 cloves	garlic, thinly sliced		

Peel and cut the potatoes length-wise into thirds. Slice the potatoes into 1/16-inch or thinner pieces (a mandoline is great for this, but do be careful.)

In a large skillet, heat the olive oil over medium-high heat. Add the garlic and cook only until it turns a roasted color, less than a minute. Add the onion and cook until translucent. Layer the potatoes on top of the onions and garlic, with a sprinkle of salt and pepper on each layer. Mix all together and continue to cook, stirring every 2 minutes until it begins turning a golden color. Remove the pan from the stove and drain off any excess oil.

Adjust the heat to medium and pour in the eggs. Mix to combine and continue to cook for 2 to 3 minutes, just until the eggs begin to set.

Place a lid on the skillet until the center of the eggs is set (jiggle the skillet as a good test) and no longer looks moist.

Remove the tortilla from the heat and allow cool for a few minutes. Give the skillet a good shake and run a spatula around the edge to help loosen the tortilla. To plate it, simply invert the tortilla onto a large platter or run a spatula underneath the tortilla to lift and tilt out of the skillet.

This dish is most often cut into wedges and served at room temperature. It is best served with music, a crisp salad, hot bread, and good company.

KATHLEEN NETTLETON
HIBISCUS COCKTAIL
MAKES 1 quart or 4 eight-ounce cocktails

Elegantly thoughtful for gracious entertaining is a non-alcoholic, ruby-colored cocktail.

1 quart	water (half can be sparkling)
1/2 plus 1/4 cup	granulated sugar
1/2 cup	dried hibiscus flowers (or dry hibiscus tea)
1/2	lime juice, freshly squeezed
1/2	cinnamon stick (optional)
	lemon slices as garnish
	lime slices as garnish
	mint or basil as garnish

In a medium saucepan, add 2 cups of plain still water and 1/2 cup of sugar. Boil until the sugar has dissolved. Remove from heat. Stir in the dried hibiscus flowers or add twice the recommended dry prepared tea.

Cover and stand for 20 minutes. Strain into a pitcher and discard the solids. The liquid is now a concentrate and may be stored refrigerated. To serve, chill the glasses. Place the remaining 1/4 cup of sugar in a small saucer, and rotate the glass rims in the sugar. Add the remaining 2 cups of water, using either sparkling water or club soda, to the concentrate and pour over ice. Garnish with a slice of lime, basil, or mint.

GRITS & GOOD EATING

We tend to have strong opinions about peculiar things.

Like grits. Love 'em or hate 'em.

In New Orleans, we serve them from the Queen's Breakfast, a fête following a Mardi Gras Ball, to the simplest home tables.

Grits lovers like them simple; those who don't do when mascarpone is added with country butter, wild mushrooms, or crayfish tails. Think polenta–celebrated and fanciful–a prom queen. Take grits–elsewhere ignored or unadorned–a wall flower. Few cooks know that grits have great personalities. Savvy cooks know this to be true.

Grits and polenta, both ground from corn, are first cousins. Cooled, hardened grits or polenta is sliced, sauteed, or grilled, either as savory or sweet tastes. They come as instant, quick cooking, or stone ground. Most cooks prefer the quick cooking grits (not instant), or the best, stone ground. White or yellow grits is a choice of color.

They mix and mingle, asking only for the addition of butter and a little salt. Other flavor boosts include cream, milk, chicken or beef stock instead of water. Savory grits highlight cheeses and seasonings, are drizzled with gravies, and topped with garnishes. Sweet grits are as versatile. Cane or pancake syrup, fruit and jams or jellies shine.

Shapes for different recipes–easy. Pour the cooked, hot grits into an empty tin can or spread them evenly in a baking pan; cover and refrigerate until hardened. Open the bottom of the can, run a little hot water over the tin and push the cylinder of grits out onto a cutting board for slicing. Rest the bottom of the baking pan in some hot water to easily release them, and cut the grits into squares or rectangles. Pour the grits out in a thinner layer, and use cookie cutters for creativity. Make bite-sized balls with a melon scoop from a bowl of grits. Dust with flour, or not, then pan-fry or bake.

The farmer's market on Saturday morning features a truckload of Louisiana specialties. It's unsocial and unfair to pass up a sack or two of grits, rice or homemade seasonings and sauces.

Chefs Paul Prudhomme, John Folse, and Emeril Lagasse have done much to bring these specialties to America's markets. Enlightened stores offer the products. They are also available online.

These are ingredients for conjuring with–food for the soul.

CHEF TOMMY DIGIOVANNI, ARNAUD'S
3-STEP GRITS

SERVES 8

4 cups	water
1 teaspoon	salt
2 tablespoons	butter
1 cup	quick-cooking grits

Bring the water, salt and 2 tablespoons of butter to a boil in a 2-quart saucepan. Slowly stir in the grits. Lower heat and cook, stirring often, for 5 to 7 minutes, or until thick and creamy. Serve.

CHEESE GRITS

4 cups	water
1 teaspoon	salt
2 tablespoons	butter
1 cup	quick-cooking grits

Prepare as above, then add:

1/2 cup	grated Cheddar cheese (or cheese of your choice)

Add the grated cheese, cook and stir until the cheese melts the grits. Remove from heat pour into a serving dish.

FRIED CHEESE GRITS

Prepare as above, then remove from heat and cool for 2 to 3 minutes. Pour cooked grits into a greased dish or loaf pan approximately 9 x 5 inches or a straight-sided glass container about 4-inches in diameter. Cover with plastic wrap and refrigerate overnight or until solid.

At serving time, turn the grits out of the mold and slice into 1/2 inch patties.

Place seasoned flour in a plate or pie tin. Dredge patties lightly and shake off excess. Warm 1/2-cup clarified butter over medium high heat and fry the patties until golden on each side. Immediately top with a sprinkle of cheese as garnish.

CAFÉ ADELAIDE
TOMATO & GRILLED OREGANO GRITS

SERVES 6

1 quart	milk
1 quart	heavy cream
2 sticks (8 ounces)	unsalted butter
1/4 cup	onion, finely chopped
2 cloves	garlic, finely chopped
1 tablespoon	shallot, finely chopped
2 cups	stone ground grits
1 teaspoon	salt
1 teaspoon	pepper
4 cups	fresh peeled and chopped and drained tomato (about 6 to 7 whole tomatoes)
1 cup	tomato paste
1/4 bunch	fresh oregano

Using a large saucepan, boil the milk and heavy cream and set aside. In a separate large skillet, melt the butter over a medium flame and stir the chopped vegetables until translucent. Add and toast the grits for 2 minutes. Add the milk and cream to the grits mixture and stir. Season and cook over a low flame for about 1 1/2 hours, stirring occasionally. In a small saucepan over a medium to low flame, cook the fresh tomato until soft, puree in a blender until smooth and combine with the tomato paste. Stir evenly into grits. Grill the oregano leaves, finely chop, and stir into grits. Taste for seasoning.

Creamy Corn Grits

Chef Greg Reggio swears there is no cheese. Chef Gary Darling promises he has not added a secret ingredient to the recipe and Chef Hans Limburg would never contradict his partners. The Taste Buds: Three chefs, one mission.

SERVES 8

2 ears	fresh corn
1	tablespoon butter
2 cups	water
2 cups	heavy cream
1 cup	yellow quick 5-minute grits
1/2 teaspoon	salt
	green onion for garnish

Grill the corn, which may be done in advance and kept covered in the refrigerator until ready to use. Shuck the husks and butter the ears.

Grill over an open fire (preferably charcoal) until the kernels are dark brown here and there. Cool the corn. Slice the kernels off the cob, stem end down on a cutting board and slicing downward.

In a 2-quart saucepan combine the water, cream, and butter. Bring to a light boil over a medium heat. Slowly whisk in the grits and then the corn. Stirring frequently to avoid lumps, reduce the heat to a simmer and cook 5 to 6 minutes. Add salt and pepper to taste. Garnish and serve.

NOTE: Using a skillet, the kernels brown in about a tablespoon of butter, stirring until they are the right color. Under the broiler on a sheet pan with a little butter also works. Use frozen corn only in a pinch.

DOOKY CHASE'S
BAKED GRITS & CHEESE
SERVES 6

4 cups	water
1 cup	quick grits
1/2 teaspoon	salt
1/4 cup	milk
1	egg, beaten
1 cup	cheddar cheese, grated

Preheat oven to 375°F

In a medium saucepan, bring water to a rolling boil. In a steady stream, add grits and salt, stirring occasionally and boil 10 to 15minutes until just done. In a separate bowl, mix together milk, egg, and cheese. Add to grits, stirring well until cheese has completely melted. Using a medium-sized buttered baking dish, pour in mixture and bake for 15 minutes.

Serve with buttered, toasted French bread

Plain buttered grits are also excellent. Simply follow the package directions.

MR. B'S BISTRO
STONE-GROUND GRITS

Stone-ground grits are night and day from instant grits. Many chefs and good cooks won't allow instant grits on the premises. Stone-ground grits have more of the kernel of the corn and their texture when cooked is heartier. Instant grits will not work in this recipe.

SERVES 6

2 cups	heavy cream
2 cups	whole milk
1 cup	stone-ground grits
1/3 cup	mascarpone cheese
to taste	kosher salt and freshly ground
	black pepper

In a medium saucepan bring cream and milk to a simmer over moderately low heat. Whisk in grits and cook, stirring often, and checking for doneness about 30 to 45 minutes. Stir in cheese and season with salt and pepper.

Tucked away in a corner of the Bywater neighborhood just past the French Quarter, Feelings is a hometown secret. Owner Jim Baird has been serving local recipes for more than 30 years at his establishment. A haven for creative types; artists, musicians, actors, and writers, they revel in the laid back atmosphere.

It is easy to imagine a celebrity at the next table. Guests include both the famous and infamous, too private to be named. New Orleanians would never interrupt someone, no matter how well-known. That would be strictly against our code of behavior.

Casually funky and fun, Feelings embraces a romantic courtyard for lazy afternoons and quiet cocktails.

The dining room is beamed with salvaged wood from barges that hauled provisions down the Mississippi River. The barges were then broken up to be sold for their lumber value.

JIM BAIRD, FEELINGS
GRILLADES & GRITS

Grillade translates from French as grilled meat and may be prepared from beef, veal or pork. Grillades and grits is most frequently served at brunch and makes a fine dinner, stepping up and down all rungs of the social ladder. Feelings uses veal rounds, lightly pounded thin, seasoned and quickly sauteed. Another characteristic of the recipe is the abundance of tomatoes in the sauce.

SERVES 4

GRILLADES

4 tablespoons	butter		3 ounces	tomato paste
1/2 cup	vegetable oil			(1/2 of a 6 ounce can)
2 tablespoons	flour		1	bay leaf
1	onion, chopped		1/2 teaspoon	fresh or dried thyme,
1	green bell pepper, chopped			chopped
1	red bell pepper, chopped		1/2 tablespoon	parsley, chopped
1 tablespoon	fresh garlic, pureed		1 tablespoon	granulated sugar
to taste	black pepper		1 tablespoon	Worcestershire sauce
to taste	cayenne pepper		1 tablespoon	Pick-A-Pepper sauce
to taste	Crystal Hot Sauce		1 teaspoon	salt
4 cups	sliced mushrooms, divided		dash	Tabasco
1/4 cup	green onion, sliced		8	veal cutlets (1 1/4 to
3 cups	tomato sauce			1 1/2 pounds total)
1/2 cup	red wine			pounded thin
1 1/2 cups	beef broth			

FOR THE SAUCE

In a cast iron skillet over a medium low flame, combine the butter, oil and flour to make a light roux. Stir continuously until it is a light tan color. Stir the chopped onions, peppers and pureed garlic into the roux. Cook until soft and translucent. Season with black pepper, cayenne pepper and Crystal Hot Sauce. Add 2 cups of the sliced mushrooms and 1/4 cup of green onion and stir in the tomato sauce, the red wine and beef broth until well combined. Add the remaining ingredients. Simmer for at least 30 minutes, adding broth or wine, if needed, for desired consistency.

FOR THE GRILLADES

Place the veal cutlets between two sheets of waxed paper. Pound thin. Add a few tablespoons of butter to a hot skillet, brown the veal cutlets for two to three minutes on each side. Top with the sauce and simmer for 10 minutes.

Serve with your favorite cheese grits recipe *(page 42)*.

BREAKFAST SHRIMP
& BAKED CHEESE GRITS

Say "shrimp and grits", most people are pleased. If it is said in reference to Chef Leah Chase's version, you'll see smiles—even grins. There's an idle debate about where the dish was created, but here we believe it is as original as Leah. Served with her special baked grits; people smile and dance all the way to the table.

SERVES 6

4	tomatoes (very ripe)		2 pounds	medium to large shrimp, peeled and deveined
1 quart	boiling water		1/2 teaspoon	salt
1 4-ounce stick	unsalted butter		1/4 teaspoon	cayenne pepper
1/2 cup	onion, diced		2 fresh	basil leaves, chopped
1/2 cup	bell peppers, diced		1 tablespoon	parsley, chopped
2 cloves	fresh garlic, fine chopped			

In a 2 quart sized pot 1/2 full, bring water to a boil. Using a slotted spoon or tongs, dip tomatoes into the boiling water for 15 to 20 seconds. Remove, rinse under cold water, slide off peels, core, seed and chop. Set aside.

In a large saucepan over medium heat, melt butter. Add onions, green peppers, and garlic. Stir (saute) until onions are transparent (clear.) Add tomatoes; shrimp, and paprika, salt, cayenne pepper, and basil leaves. Stir 10 minutes or until shrimp are cooked (pink throughout,)

Serve over grits (recipe on p 45) and garnish with chopped parsley.

NOTE: Heads on unpeeled shrimp are about 1/3 to 1/2 more weight than peeled shrimp.

Chef Leah Chase has been cooking for more than fifty years and is nationally known as the Queen of Creole Cooking and for her down-to-earth sense of humor.

Her smile and gracious manner let you know immediately that she's a lady—a lady to be reckoned with. Her charitable, civic and professional efforts have been repeatedly recognized, although she seeks nothing but to feed her guests properly and serve her community.

She was one of the seventy-five women featured in "I Dream A World: Portraits of Black Women Who Changed America," she received the National Candace Award as one of the ten most outstanding black women in the country, was the recipient of the New Orleans Times-Picayune's Loving Cup, and was given the Ella Brennan Savoir Faire Award for Excellence by the National Federation of Chefs. The James Beard Society has also honored her. She's authored two cookbooks and an autobiography.

Leah has received awards from the Anti-Defamation League, and the NAACP, as well as honorary doctorate degrees from Holy Cross College in New Orleans and Madonna College in Detroit.

The most significant honor she's received is the title Great-Grandmother.

Margo Landen

Mr. B's stands for Brennan's, another mighty offshoot of the restaurant group – the Commander's Palace side of the family, if you're keeping score. Managing Partner Cindy Brennan works closely with Executive Chef Michelle McRaney to provide Creole-style specialties in the French Quarter.

CHEF MICHELLE MCRANEY, MR. B'S BISTRO
GUMBO YA-YA

Legend says that the term "gumbo ya-ya" was a French-based dialect spoken in New Orleans during the 1800s. The late New Orleans author Lyle Saxon borrowed it for the title of his book of Louisiana folk tales. Another school of thought says that "gumbo ya-ya" referred to the chattering of women while they cooked in 19th century New Orleans. Cindy Brennan, proprietor of Mister B's Bistro in the French Quarter, says the restaurant's gumbo ya-ya is the best-selling dish on the menu.

MAKES about 6 quarts

1 pound (4 sticks)	unsalted butter	1 teaspoon	freshly ground black pepper
3 cups	all-purpose flour	1 teaspoon	dried hot red-pepper flakes
2	red bell peppers, diced	1 teaspoon	chile powder
2	green bell peppers, diced	1 teaspoon	dried thyme
2	medium onions, diced	1 tablespoon	minced garlic
2	celery stalks, diced	2	bay leaves
1 1/4 gallons (20 cups)	chicken stock	1	3-1/2-pound chicken, roasted and boned
1 pound	andouille sausage, cut into 1/4-inch-thick slices		hot sauce to taste
2 tablespoons	Creole seasoning		boiled or steamed rice
2 tablespoons	kosher or sea salt plus additional to taste		

*Andouille is a lean and spicy pork sausage made in south Louisiana. Any good-quality pork sausage, such as kielbasa, may be substituted.

Begin by making a dark roux. In a 12-quart stock pot melt the butter over low heat. Gradually add 1 cup of the flour, stirring constantly with a wooden spoon, and continue cooking, stirring constantly, for 30 seconds. Add 1 more cup of flour and stir constantly for 30 seconds. Add the remaining cup flour and stir constantly for 30 seconds. Continue to cook the roux, stirring constantly, until it is the color of dark mahogany, about 45 minutes to 1 hour.

Add the red and green bell peppers to the roux and stir constantly for 30 seconds. Add the onions and celery and stir constantly for 30 seconds. Gradually add stock to the roux, stirring constantly with a wooden spoon to prevent lumps. Add the andouille sausage, Creole seasoning, salt, black pepper, red pepper flakes, chile powder, thyme, garlic and bay leaves, and bring to a boil. Simmer gumbo, uncovered, for 45 minutes, skimming off any fat and stirring occasionally.

Add chicken meat and simmer 15 minutes. Adjust seasoning with salt and hot sauce.

Serve over rice.

ARNAUD'S
OYSTER SOUP

SERVES 6

3 1/2 cups	water		1/8 teaspoon	ground red pepper
2 dozen	freshly shucked oysters, drained		1	bay leaf
1/2 cup	chopped celery		3/4 cup	heavy cream
1/2 cup	chopped green onions		2 cups	milk
1/2 cup	chopped onion		1/4 cup	butter
1 tablespoon	butter, melted		1/2 cup	all purpose flour
1/2 teaspoon	finely chopped garlic		1 teaspoon	salt
1/8 teaspoon	dried thyme		1/4 teaspoon	ground white pepper

Bring water to a boil in a medium saucepan. Add oysters and cook for 3 minutes. Remove oysters with a slotted spoon and reserve 3 cups liquid. Set both aside.

In a Dutch oven over medium heat, cook celery, green onions and onions in 1 tablespoon butter, stirring constantly until tender. Stir in 2-1/2 cups reserved liquid, garlic, thyme, red pepper and bay leaf; bring to a boil. Stir in heavy cream, reduce heat and simmer 5 minutes. Stir in milk and return to a simmer.

Melt 1/4-cup butter in a small saucepan over low heat. Add flour, stirring until smooth. Cook 1 minute, stirring constantly, then about 3 minutes or until smooth (mixture will be very thick.)

Gradually add flour mixture to milk mixture, stirring with a wire whisk until blended. Add oysters, salt and white pepper. Cook until thoroughly heated. Remove from heat, discard bay leaf.

Arnaud's lasting success can be attributed in part to the constancy of its owners: It has known only two families in its years of operation, from the colorful founder "Count" Arnaud Cazenave to Archie A. Casbarian.

When the late Archie A. Casbarian and Jane, his wife, acquired the establishment in 1979, first priority was returning Arnaud's original glamour. The chandeliers, iron columns, and cypress paneling were restored. The old ceiling fans also stayed. The wall of opaque, pebbled glass windows overlooking Bienville Street was replaced by sparkling beveled glass. The renaissance of Arnaud's had finally begun.

In a city known for its culinary excellence and abundance of fine restaurants, few establishments have achieved worldwide acclaim. Arnaud's stands as a monument to the enduring allure of tradition with a menu founded in the Creole classics.

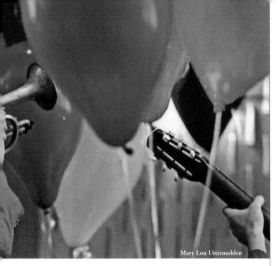

New Orleans has Mardi Gras Queens and Kings, but also crown chefs and restaurateurs. Ella Brennan is considered the Queen of New Orleans cuisine. These titles are not lightly bestowed in a city where restaurateurs and chefs are icons and royalty. Receiving the James Beard Foundation's Lifetime Achievement honors, she quipped, "I didn't know they gave out awards for having fun."

Ella inspired and instigated many novel traditions, as a young woman at Brennan's of Royal Street then later at Commander's Palace.

She knew guests enjoyed sampling different tastes. The result of that small observation is the now traditional trio of soups each served in a demitasse cup.

One of Ella's many talents was nurturing Commander's young chefs to national prominence: Paul Prudhomme, Emeril Lagasse, the late Jamie Shannon, and now Tory McPhail.

The family's flagship restaurant is now co-managed by her daughter Ti Adelaide Martin and niece Lally Brennan.

CHEF TORY MCPHAIL, COMMANDER'S PALACE
TURTLE SOUP

Turtle meat is usually sold frozen in 2 1/2-pound portions, so this recipe is written to use that quantity. The meat freezes well (as does the soup) and can be ordered by mail or on the Internet.

SERVES 6

12 tablespoons	butter	1 cup	all-purpose flour
2 1/2 pounds	turtle meat,* medium dice	1750-milliliter	bottle dry sherry
	kosher salt and freshly	1 tablespoon	hot sauce, or to taste
	ground pepper to taste	1/4 cup	Worcestershire sauce
2	medium onions,	2	large lemons, juiced
	medium dice	3 cups	fresh tomatoes, peeled,
6	celery stalks, medium dice		seeded and coarsely
1	large head garlic, cloves		chopped
	peeled and minced	10 ounces	fresh spinach, washed
3	bell peppers, any color,		thoroughly, stems removed
	medium dice		and coarsely chopped
1 tablespoon	ground dried thyme	6	medium eggs, hard-boiled
1 tablespoon	ground dried oregano		and chopped into large pieces
4	whole bay leaves		
2 quarts	veal stock		

*Beef or a combination of lean beef and veal stew meat may be substituted for the turtle meat.

Melt 4 tablespoons of the butter in a large soup pot over medium to high heat. Brown the meat in the hot butter. Season with salt and pepper, and cook for about 18 to 20 minutes, or until the liquid is almost evaporated.

Add the onions, celery, garlic and peppers, stirring constantly. Then add the thyme, oregano and bay leaves and sauve for 20 to 25 minutes, until the vegetables have caramelized. Add the stock, bring to a boil, lower the heat and simmer uncovered for 30 minutes, periodically skimming away any fat that rises to the top.

While the stock is simmering, make a roux in a separate pot: Melt the remaining 8 tablespoons of butter over medium heat in a small saucepan and add the flour a little at a time, stirring constantly with a wooden spoon. Be careful not to burn the roux. After all the flour has been added, cook for about 3 minutes until the roux smells nutty, is pale in color, and has the consistency of wet sand. Set aside until the soup is ready.

Using a whisk, vigorously stir the roux into the soup a little at a time to prevent lumping. Simmer for about 25 minutes. Stir to prevent sticking on the bottom.

Add the sherry and bring the liquid to a boil. Add the hot sauce and worcestershire and simmer, skimming any fat or foam that rises to the top. Add juice from the lemons and the tomatoes, and return to a simmer. Add the spinach and the chopped egg. Return to a simmer and adjust salt and pepper as needed.

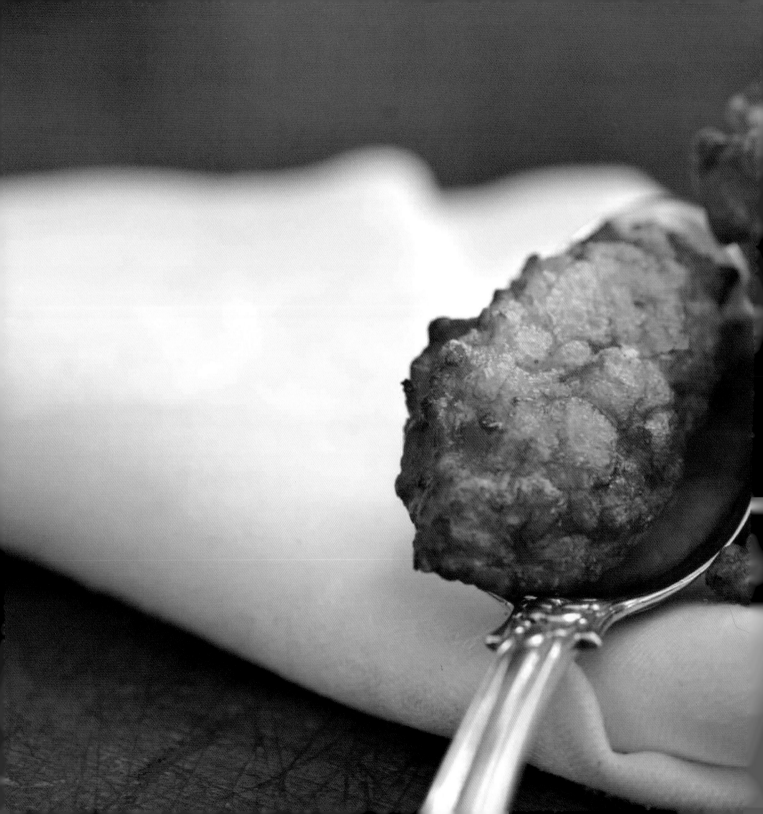

BREADS, PANCAKES & WAFFLES

The legend, myth–perhaps true or not–is that our water makes New Orleans French bread unique. Many have tried and failed to make it in other places. Many blame the water. Consider the Big Easy atmosphere that helps the yeast rise and the hands of New Orleanians kneading the dough. It could be spirit.

Fresh French bread becomes po boys. Sliced or torn, it is served at almost every meal. Someone offers a baguette, so a guest can pull off a chunk. That makes crumbs. Tradition says company must leave crumbs to follow, so they will return.

Leftover French bread turns into lost bread–bread lost is found again as pain perdue. It also becomes bread pudding. The crumbs are hoarded for stuffing, breading, and seasoning. Breads and biscuits are slathered, dipped, fried, crumbled, and dressed to reappear. Not much is wasted. We enjoy spending time at the table, and we enjoy talking about food. Neither of those things is wasted.

Possibly the only bread sort of thing never leftover is beignets or rice calas. Served crispy hot, they're gone before the café au lait.

Unlike beignets, calas are not nearly as well known. Calas, almost a forgotten New Orleans specialty, is made from–once again–leftover rice. These fritter-like treats are reappearing in homes and restaurants.

Writer Lolis Elie, who knows these things, says beignets are restaurant fare and calas were street food. African-American street vendors carried baskets of fresh, hot calas throughout the Vieux Carré in the 1800s. African-American cooks made–some still do–calas in celebration of Mardi Gras Day (the day before Lent begins), Christmas, or a Catholic First Communion.

Beignets and calas origins may be African, French, or the Celtic. No one seems to have bragging rights to beignets. Many cultures have their own versions of fritters, fried pastry, and other donut-like treats.

Pancakes, waffles and biscuits are enjoyed everywhere. These New Orleans-style brunch specialties play off variations on a theme, with notes of bright flavor, much like jazz music.

We claim both beignets and calas, rightly so. We claim jazz music, too.

Poppy has a love affair with local food. As a result, she authored the wildly successful "Crescent City Farmer's Market Cookbook."

Her motto "Eat it to Save It," has been instrumental in stimulating interest in endangered foods such as calas and Creole cream cheese.

Active in the Southern Foodways Alliance, Poppy is sought after for speaking and demonstration engagements.

As a cook, she bested Bobby Flay in a gumbo throwdown and stars in a variety of showcase radio and television productions.

POPPY TOOKER
CALAS

Eighteenth-century street vendors called "CALAS! CALAS, TOUT CHAUD! Calas, all hot!" carrying baskets of fried rice pastries through the French Quarter. Calas, dusted with confectioner's sugar, honey, pancake syrup or drizzled with Steen's cane syrup is a time-honored treat in the Creole community, particularly in the predominantly African American Treme neighborhood. The calas ladies were able to walk from Treme to the French Quarter for their morning rounds.

Calas may also be made as a savory by excluding the sugar ingredient, then adding seasonings and bits of leftover meat.

Heat oil to 350°F.

A thermometer is a handy gauge unless you are Poppy Tooker, who successfully intuits when they are done. Teaspoon-size calas use 350°F oil. Tablespoon-size calas may brown too quickly. Lower the oil temperature by 10°F and they will cook through.

MAKES 2 dozen

6 tablespoons	flour		2	eggs, beaten
3 heaping tablespoons	sugar		1/4 teaspoon	vanilla
2 teaspoons	baking powder			vegetable oil for frying
1/4 teaspoon	salt			Confectioners' sugar, honey, or
	Pinch of nutmeg			Steen's Cane Syrup for topping
2 cups	cooked rice			

In a medium size bowl, combine the flour, sugar, baking powder, and salt. Using a separate bowl, thoroughly mix the rice, beaten eggs, and vanilla. Add the dry ingredients to the wet mixture and combine. In a heavy bottomed skillet or fryer, bring the oil to 360°F. Carefully drop teaspoons of batter into the hot oil without crowding and fry until brown on one side, 1 to 2 minutes. Using tongs or a spatula, turn and brown the second side. When frying several batches, let the oil cool back to the proper temperature. Using a slotted spoon or sieve, scoop out the loose browned bits. Drain on paper towels. Sprinkle with powdered sugar or drizzle with syrup or honey, and serve hot, immediately.

CHEF MARY SONNIER, THE UPTOWNER
GRUYÈRE BISCUITS
& HAM CREOLLAISE

It was at K-Paul's Louisiana Kitchen that chefs Mary Blanchard and Greg Sonnier fell in love with each other and the restaurant business. Gabrielle Restaurant followed soon, named after their daughter. With their talent and passion for Creole cooking, the Sonniers' continue enhance New Orleans reputation by producing special extraordinary food and hospitality. Chef Mary also hosts The Chef Show on a local public radio station.

MAKES 12 Biscuits or 30 Mini Biscuits

BISCUITS

2 1/4 cups	self-rising flour		1 cup	gruyère cheese, grated
1/2 teaspoon	salt		1 tablespoon	flour
1/4 teaspoon	cayenne pepper		1	egg yolk
3/4 cup	unsalted butter		2 tablespoons	cream
1/2 cup	cold buttermilk		to taste	coarse salt
1	egg		2 tablespoons	gruyère cheese, grated

Preheat oven to 425°F.

In a large bowl, combine the flour, salt and cayenne and mix well.

Cut in the butter and work with your fingertips until the mixture is coarse (like small peas and not lumpy). Mix the cold buttermilk and egg in a small bowl. Make a well in the center of the flour mixture and slowly stir in the buttermilk and egg mixture, until all of the ingredients are thoroughly moistened.

Dust the cheese with 1 tablespoon of flour and then fold into the biscuit mix. Turn the mixture onto a floured board and knead gently (4 or 5 times). Roll the dough to 1/4-inch thickness and cut with a 2 1/2-inch biscuit cutter (1-inch cutter for mini appetizer-sized biscuits).

Place the cut biscuits (sides touching) on a parchment-lined cookie sheet. Combine the egg yolk and cream in a small bowl. Brush the biscuits with the egg/cream mixture, sprinkle with a little coarse salt and an extra 2 tablespoons of cheese.

Bake for approximately 20 minutes, or until golden brown.

CREOLAISSE

1/2 cup	Blue Plate Mayonnaise		1 teaspoon	Worcestershire sauce
1/4 cup	Zatarain's Creole Mustard			

In a small bowl, mix everything together with a whisk until smooth.

ASSEMBLY

In a skillet, fry about 1 to 1 1/2 pounds of sliced ham in a bit of butter. Put a couple of slices of fried ham between each biscuit that has been smeared with Creollaise.

MAKE AHEAD NOTE: You can assemble the biscuits and ham ahead of serving; warm in a 350°F oven, then using a squirt bottle, squeeze the Creollaise on right before serving.

NANCY CALHOUN
BRUNCH PUNCH
MAKES 24 8-ounce servings

"Miss Nancy" delights guests with new twists on old favorites. Her non-alcoholic recipe is colorful, and refreshing. Vary it based on the season. Select fresh fruit and specialty ices in contrasting colors and complimentary flavors.

1	orange
1 pint	strawberries
1 pint	blueberries
1	melon
1	lemon
1	lime
1 quart	lemon ice (flavors optional)
6 quarts	ginger ale, chilled
	Mint for garnish

Prepare fruit smaller than bite-size. Using a vegetable peeler or citrus zester, cut ribbons of skin from the orange, lemon and lime and set the fruit aside. Cut the ribbons into pieces that curl, knot, or twist. Cut the citrus into 1/4-inch slices. Segment the orange and cut into 1/2-inch pieces. Hull and cut berries into halves or quarters. Make melon balls.

Place lemon ice in a large punch bowl, add ginger ale, the fruit pieces, and float garnishes of decorative twists, slices and mint.

BRANDY MILK PUNCH

MAKES 1 cocktail

2 ounces	brandy
1 ounce	simple syrup *(page 23)*
1/2 teaspoon	pure vanilla extract
1 1/2 ounces	milk
	Freshly grated nutmeg, for garnish

Combine all the ingredients in a cocktail shaker with ice and shake vigorously. Strain into a rocks glass filled with ice. Garnish with a light dusting of freshly grated nutmeg and serve immediately.

CHEF TORY MCPHAIL, COMMANDER'S PALACE
HUCKLEBERRY PANCAKES

Chef Tory has a talent for presentation, taking the familiar and elevating it to an unexpected point of view. At Commander's Palace, he follows the great chef Paul Prudhomme, then the late Jamie Shannon as executive chef for managing partners Ti Martin and Lally Brennan. They pay special attention to the heart and soul of the restaurant; the kitchen and the dishes created there. Commander's cuisine reflects both of the city's Creole and American heritages as well as dishes of Commander's own creating.

His huckleberry pancake is as colorful and as cheerful as Commander's brunch balloons and spirited jazz.

SERVES 4 to 6

2	eggs		1 tablespoon	kosher salt
3 tablespoons	butter, melted		3 tablespoons	granulated sugar
1/4 teaspoon	vanilla extract		2 tablespoons	baking powder
1 1/2 cups	cake flour		1 to 2 teaspoons	vegetable oil

In a medium bowl combine eggs, butter and vanilla extract. In another medium bowl, mix flour, salt, sugar and baking powder.

Gently whisk the egg mixture with the dry ingredients until just combined (a few lumps may remain). Do not over work.

Allow mixture to rest 1/2 to 1 hour before cooking.

To cook, heat a 12-inch nonstick skillet, heavy bottomed skillet or a griddle over medium heat for 3 to 5 minutes. Add 1 teaspoon of oil to coat the bottom of the skillet evenly. Pour 1/4 cup of batter onto 3 to 4 spots on the skillet and cook the pancake until large bubbles begin to appear, about 1 1/2 to 2 minutes. Using a spatula, flip the pancakes over and cook until golden brown on the second side. Repeat with remaining batter, using remaining 1 teaspoon of vegetable oil as necessary.

SAUCE

1 ounce	white chocolate, chopped			confectioner's sugar to garnish
2 ounces	huckleberries			honeycomb for garnish
	mint leaves to garnish		1 ounce	candied pecans *(page 93)*

Sprinkle pancakes with white chocolate and huckleberries and garnish with sprig of mint leaves. Dust with confectioners' sugar. Candied pecans may be served with pancakes.

DR. TLALOC ALFEREZ
PAIN PERDUE

Dr. Tlaloc Alferez is famed throughout the South as a physician of consequence and skill. She takes after her father, the late artist Enrique Alferez, in creativity and inventiveness. While he made art, she makes use of her talents both in her practice and in her kitchen. Saving leftover French bread as pain perdue is one of her many specialties. A coincidence, he created the magnificent bas reliefs and bronze doors at Charity Hospital.

This popular dish was created by the Creoles as another way of making use of leftovers. While French bread is preferable, Italian or any other dense bread will work well. Loaf bread slices can be used, but they are just not the same. The recipe can be dressed up or down, as desired.

SERVES 6

6	eggs	powdered sugar, chopped roasted
3 tablespoons	granulated sugar	pecans, honey, pancake or cane syrup,
1 tablespoon	vanilla extract	for toppings
1 cup	milk	
1/2 teaspoon	ground cinnamon	applesauce, for garnish, if desired
1/4 teaspoon	ground nutmeg	
12 slices	French, Italian or other	sliced or stewed fresh fruit such as
	white bread, stale	strawberries, apples, pears, or
	3/4-inch to 1-inch thick	bananas, if desired
1/2 cup (4 ounces, 1 stick)	unsalted butter, melted,	
	or vegetable oil	

In a large, wide and shallow bowl that is larger than the slices of bread, beat the eggs, sugar, vanilla, milk, cinnamon, nutmeg and milk, until smooth and evenly colored. If using a French bread baguette, slice on a diagonal instead of straight up and down, for a larger surface area.

One or two at a time, soak the bread slices in the custard mixture for a little less than a minute on each side, so the bread absorbs some of the liquid. Caution: the bread will get soggy and fall apart if left in the liquid too long.

Preheat the oven to the lowest heat and place a paper towel-lined platter and six brunch plates inside to warm.

Heat a large skillet or a griddle over high heat until a drop of water pops and skitters across the surface. Brush generously with the butter and add one batch of bread (how many slices per batch will depend on the size of the pan; do not crowd the slices). Fry for a minute or two on each side until golden brown and crispy. Transfer the finished pain perdu to the platter in the oven to keep warm while you fry the remaining slices. Add more butter as necessary and note that as more slices are cooked, you will have to lower the temperature to keep them from burning.

Sprinkle with powdered sugar or chopped roasted pecans, or drizzle with honey, syrup, or applesauce. Scatter with fresh fruit, if desired, and serve.

PEGGY SCOTT LABORDE & ERROL LABORDE
THE LOUISIANA PURCHASE

What better way to toast that all-important purchase way back in 1803 that included New Orleans!

Ingredients include American whiskey, French Grand Marnier, that delightful orange liquor; Spanish sherry and Florida grapefruit juice (a reminder that the Florida Parishes weren't part of the Purchase but a later addition).

MAKES 1 drink

1 ounce	Grand Marnier
1 ounce	rye whiskey (Old Overholt preferred)
1 ounce	Spanish sherry
5 ounces	grapefruit juice (Ruby Red)

Shake well with cracked ice and pour into Old-Fashioned Cocktail glass. Garnish with a cherry.

SAZERAC ROOM
ROOSEVELT HOTEL

SAZERAC

MAKES 1 cocktail

3 ounces	rye whiskey
3/4 ounce	simple syrup *(page 23)*
to taste	Peychaud bitters (or substitute absinthe or Herbsaint)
lemon twist	for garnish

Chill an old-fashioned glass by filling it with ice and letting it sit while preparing the rest of the drink.

In a separate mixing glass, muddle the simple syrup and Peychaud bitters together.

Add the rye whiskey and ice to the bitters mixture and stir.

Discard the ice in the chilled glass and rinse it with absinthe (or substitute Herbsaint) by pouring a small amount into the glass, swirling it around and discarding the liquid.

Strain the whiskey mixture from the mixing glass into the old fashioned glass.

Garnish with a lemon twist.

ERIN HICKS MILLER
PAIN PERDUE BANANAS FOSTER

An award-winning author, designer and photographer, Erin covers the food world from New Orleans to New York; Corpus Christi to California. Her passion is developing lush books and video projects as toasts to the culinary arts. Texas is home plate with frequent stays in the Big Easy. Pain perdue or lost bread (some call it French toast), is another versatile dish. Erin has created a skinny, lower calorie recipe with a Bananas Foster flair, as a guide toward devising your own flavors using her basic

SERVES 2 to 4

1	egg, beaten or 1/4 cup egg substitute		1/4-1/2 cup	walnuts or pecans, chopped
2 tablespoons	coconut, almond or soy milk		1 large	banana, sliced diagonally into 8 slices
2 tablespoons	rum (or use non-alcoholic rum flavoring)		2 tablespoons	light maple or cane syrup
2 teaspoons	clarified butter			
8 slices	French bread baguette (3/4-inch thick) sliced diagonally			

In a small bowl, combine the egg, coconut milk and rum. Stir well with a whisk. Place the bread slices in a single layer in a large shallow dish. Pour the milk mixture over the bread. Let stand for about 3 to 5 minutes, or until the milk is absorbed. Press one side of the bread into the chopped nuts and set aside.

Spray a large cast-iron skillet with a little cooking spray and melt 1/2 teaspoon of clarified butter over medium high heat. Arrange 4 bread slices in the pan and cook for 2 to 3 minutes on each side or until the bread is golden brown. Remove from the pan and keep warm. Repeat the procedure with remaining 1/2 teaspoon of butter and bread slices.

In a small nonstick skillet, heat the remaining teaspoon of clarified butter over medium high heat. Cook the banana slices for about 2 minutes on both sides, then deglaze the pan with the syrup. Top the nut-crusted side of each slice of bread with a banana slice. Drizzle with more maple or cane syrup, if desired.

CHEF EMAN LOUBIER, DANTE'S KITCHEN

PAN BREAD

Dante's serves in individual skillets. We used a 10″ cast iron skillet and served as a pie-shaped slices right out of the pan. The bread should be cooked through, but more moist than most breads or cakes.

SERVES 8 to 12

3	eggs	1 cup	cornmeal
2 cups	buttermilk	3/4 cup	sugar
1 1/2 tablespoons	sour cream	1 tablespoon	baking powder
1 1/2 tablespoons	molasses	1 tablespoon	baking soda
1/2 tablespoon	melted butter	1 teaspoon	salt
1 cup	all-purpose flour		

Preheat the oven to 400°F. Grease 10-inch heavy cast iron skillet and set aside.

In a very large bowl, beat the eggs. Add the buttermilk, sour cream, molasses and whisk well to combine.

In a separate large bowl, combine the flour, cornmeal, sugar, baking powder, baking soda and salt.

Add the dry mixture to the wet mixture, stirring well. Transfer the batter to the prepared skillet or pan.

Bake uncovered on the middle rack until golden brown for approximately 20 to 25 minutes. Set the timer, and gently rotate the skillet at 10 minutes, so it browns and cooks evenly.

Insert a toothpick to check doneness. Top with whipped cream if desired. See page 74.

PECAN & BANANA PANCAKES

SERVES 8 to 12

3	bananas	4 cups	buttermilk
4 1/2 cups	all purpose flour	4	eggs, beaten
1/2 tablespoon	baking soda		Oil for griddle
1 1/2 tablespoons	baking powder		Butter for garnish
1 cup	granulated sugar		Toasted pecans for garnish
1 tablespoon	salt		

Preheat oven to 350°F.

Leave the bananas in their peel, Score the skin in a two-inch slash on each edge. Place on a baking sheet and bake in a 350°F oven for 25 minutes. Set aside and allow to cool.

Peel the bananas. In a large bowl, thoroughly mash the pulp with a fork or potato masher. Add the buttermilk and beaten eggs, mixing them with the banana pulp.

(recipe continued at right)

(recipe continued from left)

In a separate bowl, combine the dry ingredients.

Add the wet mixture to the dry mix gently and do not over mix. The batter should be lumpy, which makes a lighter pancake.

Heat the griddle or pan to medium. Lightly oil the surface and pour 1/4 cup circles, not touching, of the batter on the surface. Cook until bubbles form on the edges, then using a spatula, turn over and cook until golden brown.

In a small pot over medium heat, warm the cane syrup until heated through. Top the pancakes with butter drizzle the syrup and garnish with toasted pecans. Serve additional butter, syrup, and pecans on the side.

CHEF MATT REGAN, JOHN BESH'S LÜKE
PECAN & BLUEBERRY PANCAKES

Lüke is John Besh's tribute to the brasseries that are found in virtually every Paris neighborhood. The menus, like those in each of Besh's multiple restaurants, are filled with full-flavored and imaginative treatments of traditional French and New Orleans dishes.

SERVES 6

2 cups	flour		1 stick (4 ounces)	butter, melted
1 tablespoon	baking powder		2 cups	blueberries, divided
1/3 cup	sugar		1 1/2 cups	Steen's cane syrup
1 1/2 cups	milk		1 cup	pecans, toasted*
1 large	egg, slightly beaten			

In a large mixing bowl, stir together the flour and baking powder. In a medium bowl, whisk milk, and egg. In a separate large mixing bowl, whisk flour, baking powder, sugar and salt. Make a well in the center of these dry ingredients, pour in the milk, butter, and egg mixture and whisk gently until just combined (a few lumps may remain). Be careful not to over mix. Add the melted butter and fold lightly. Add 1 cup blueberries.

Heat the griddle or pan to medium. Lightly butter the surface and pour 1/4 cup of the batter on to the surface. Cook until bubbles form on the edges, then turn over and cook until golden brown.

In a small pot over medium heat, add the cane syrup with 1 cup of blueberries and cook until heated through, about 5 minutes.

*Toasted pecan recipe (*page 93*).

CHEF BYRON PECK, ELIZABETH'S RESTAURANT
PRALINE BACON
MAKES 10 to 15 slices

1 pound	thick-cut bacon
2 cups	light brown sugar
1/2 cup	pecans

Preheat oven to 375°F.

Lay the bacon strips on a sheet pan, place in the oven and bake for about 10 minutes or until the bacon appears to be half-way done. Remove from the oven and allow to cool.

In a blender, combine the sugar, pecans, and process until fine. Sprinkle the sugar-pecan mixture over the bacon.

Place the sheet pan back into the oven and cook for about 10 more minutes or until caramel in color.

Watch carefully, cooking times vary based on thickness of the bacon.

LINDA ELLERBEE
SKILLET CORNBREAD

Linda Ellerbee uses this recipe (and only this recipe), which she claimed years ago from an old Houston Junior League cookbook. It's part of our traditional New Year's Day brunch. Ellerbee insists the cornbread be cooked in a very hot cast iron skillet with a handle. Her skillet is older than the recipe.

She wrote her first best-selling book *And So It Goes: Adventures in Television* while living in the French Quarter.

SERVES 6

1 cup	yellow cornmeal		1 cup	buttermilk
1/2 cup	flour		1/2 cup	sweet milk
1 teaspoon	salt		1	egg
1/2 teaspoon	baking soda		1/2 cup	cooking oil
1 tablespoon	baking powder			

Preheat oven to 450°F.

When oven is hot, grease a 10-inch or 8-inch cast iron skillet (or 8 x 8-inch pan, but the cast iron skillet is better) and place in oven to heat until very, very hot.

In a medium bowl, combine all ingredients. Stir well.

Pour batter into hot pan. Bake on the middle rack in the over for about 20 minutes, or until golden brown on top.

MICHAEL LAUVE
RAMOS GIN FIZZ

Nicknamed "The Kingfish"," Huey P. Long, then governor of Louisiana brought Sam Guarino, his bartender, from the Roosevelt Hotel to New York City in 1935, ensuring that he had a proper Ramos Gin Fizz. His slogan "Every Man A King," was created for his Share the Wealth program, continues to be valid, believes art director and illustrator Michael Lauve. He also subscribes to Long's quotation, "I used to try to get things done by saying 'please'. Now...I dynamite 'em out of my path."

Henry C. Ramos created the Gin Fizz, then known as a New Orleans Fizz, in 1888, one of New Orleans' most famous drinks at his bar in Meyer's Restaurant. The secret of its flavor and texture is orange flower water and egg whites.

MAKES 1 cocktail

1 1/2 ounces	gin
2 ounces	half and half
2 ounces	milk
1	egg white
1 tablespoon	simple syrup *(page 23)*
2 drops	orange flower water (available in the baking section of supermarkets)
1/2 teaspoon	fresh lemon juice

In a shaker half filled with ice, combine all the ingredients. Shake well for 30 seconds. Pour into a chilled glass over several cubes of ice and serve immediately.

Who could resist something as historically unique as Arnaud's? The pink Cassell diamond can be reserved for brunch or dinner in the appropriate environment. If your appetite is for different gems and jewelry, there's an abundance of the diamond's exceptional companions winking around the corner at famed M.S. Rau Antiques.

Arnaud's will have your selection presented with due fanfare and a jazz band. Simply ask that Katy Casbarian plan the event. A guest once requested her father to arrange delivery of a diamond bracelet for Adelaide Brennan. When she answered the door, a live turkey on her stoop was wearing the bracelet as a necklace.

Authentic Creole cuisine and diamonds are a Casbarian family tradition.

(recipe continued from right)
HOW TO ASSEMBLE THE WAFFLE

Place one or two waffles on a plate. Drizzle the two compotes into the waffle wells, top with whipping cream and add the syrup. Garnish with mint and fresh fruit if desired.

CHEF TOMMY DIGIOVANNI, ARNAUD'S
STUFFED WAFFLES

MAKES 6 large waffles or 12 small waffles
WAFFLES

Prepared, frozen waffles of all sizes are available at most supermarkets if you don't have a waffle iron, or the time to make them from scratch. Once cooked, waffles from this recipe may be sealed and frozen for later use.

2 cups	sifted all purpose flour	4	egg yolks, beaten
1 tablespoon	baking powder	2 cups	milk
1 tablespoon	baking soda	6 tablespoons	melted butter
1 tablespoon	granulated sugar	4	egg whites, stiffly beaten
1/2 teaspoon	ground cinnamon	1 1/2 teaspoons	vanilla extract
1/2 teaspoon	salt		

MAKES 1 1/2 cups of each
SAUCE Strawberry and Blueberry Compote

1 cup	strawberries	1 cup	blueberries
1 cup	granulated sugar	1 cup	granulated sugar
1 tablespoon	lemon juice	1 tablespoon	lemon juice

WHIPPED CREAM

1 pint	heavy cream	1 tablespoon	granulated sugar
1/2 teaspoon	vanilla extract		

Cane syrup, pancake syrup or honey

TO MAKE THE WAFFLES

In a large mixing bowl, sift together the flour, baking powder, baking soda, sugar, cinnamon, and salt. In a separate small bowl mix the milk, yolks, vanilla and butter together until well blended and stir into dry ingredients. Preheat the waffle iron.

In a medium bowl, whisk the eggs, vanilla, butter and milk until well blended. In a separate bowl, whip the egg whites until stiff. Fold into the batter. Spray the preheated waffle iron with nonstick cooking oil. Spoon batter onto the hot waffle iron, and cook until golden brown.

TO MAKE THE WHIPPED CREAM

Using a very clean metal bowl, preferably chilled, add the cream, and using an electric mixer or immersion blender, whip until it begins to thicken. Add the sugar and vanilla each in a steady stream and continue to whip until standing peaks form.

TO MAKE THE COMPOTE

Almost any fresh, seasonal fruit may be used to create a compote. In two medium-sized sauce pans, one for each berry, add all ingredients and bring to a boil over medium high heat. Continue to cook until the volume in each has reduced by 25%. Remove from heat, set aside until cool.

(recipe continued at left)

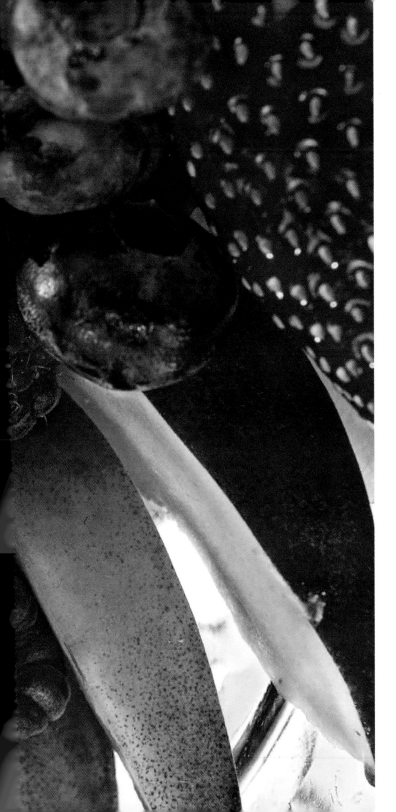

SWEETS

There's a reason we call it The Big Easy. We don't like stress. We do like desserts. In fact, nothing is more New Orleans than a sweet memory.

We Orleanians celebrate at brunch, lunch and dinner—and we crown our celebrations. An important meal isn't complete without the grand finale of a classic dessert. Even an unimportant meal (if there is such a thing) demands some dessert.

Not that you need to have brunch to celebrate dessert.

Dessert is almost mandatory with brunch. It is delicious agony to settle on just one. It's an exquisite, almost secret sweetness. In the middle of the morning. Or afternoon. Done right a New Orleans dessert will bring you to your knees.

That too is New Orleans.

As you know, our culinary heritage is based on its Spanish, French, Italian, Caribbean, African, Indian and German roots. Each group brought something to the party, and we are the better for it.

In New Orleans, we're so proud of our heritage we eat it every day. Especially at brunch.

Margo Landen

The French Quarter Festival showcases music in the streets and the World's Largest Jazz Brunch, ideal for dancing in front of Brennan's Restaurant on Royal each spring.

The Brennan's building once was the family home of young Paul Morphy, chess prodigy and master of the mid-1800s, considered the unofficial world champion. His father floored the dining room as a perfectly scaled chess board of black and white marble squares.

BRENNAN'S

BANANAS FOSTER

This is the original Bananas Foster recipe from Brennan's Restaurant. Chef Paul Blangé created it in 1951 honoring Richard Foster, who served with Owen Brennan on the New Orleans Crime Commission. Foster was a frequent guest and a close friend of the restaurant's founder.

SERVES 4

1/4 cup	(1/2 stick) butter	4	bananas, cut in half lengthwise,
1 cup	brown sugar		then halved
1/2 teaspoon	cinnamon	1/4 cup	dark rum
1/4 cup	banana liqueur	4 scoops	vanilla ice cream

Combine the butter, sugar, and cinnamon in a flame pan or skillet. Place the pan over low heat either on an alcohol burner or on top of the stove, and cook, stirring, until the sugar dissolves. Stir in the banana liqueur, then place the bananas in the pan. The banana sections will soften and begin to brown. Pour the rum into a heated ladle and carefully ignite it, holding the ladle* away from anything flammable. When the flames subside, pour the rum from the ladle into the pan and stir. Lift the bananas out of the pan and place four pieces over each portion of ice cream. Generously spoon warm sauce over the top of the ice cream and serve immediately.

NOTE: Flame cooking requires diligence, awareness, safety and caution. Never flame the liqueur in the bowl, always use a ladle. It is best to perform the ceremony on a side cart, away from yourself, the guests, intake vents and draperies. After all, you are playing with fire.

CHEF MICHAEL GOTTLIEB, REDFISH GRILL
DOUBLE CHOCOLATE
BREAD PUDDING
WITH TWO CHOCOLATE SAUCES & ALMOND BARK

SERVES 8 to 12

1 piece	day-old New Orleans-style French bread* about 23 inches long and cut into 1/2-inch cubes with crust on	1/4 pounds (3 1/2 cups)	semi-sweet chocolate chips
		8	eggs
3 cups	heavy cream	*(the following recipes are on page 92)*	
1/2 cup	milk	1 recipe	chocolate sauce, for serving
1 3/4 cups	granulated sugar, divided	1 recipe	white chocolate sauce, for serving
12-inch-long	piece of vanilla bean, scraped and seeded	8 to 12 pieces	almond bark, for garnish

NOTE: For the best results, refrigerate the uncooked bread pudding overnight before baking. Save time by preparing the sauces as well and refrigerate them.

*If New Orleans-style French bread is not available, you can get similar results using a sugarless, natural-yeast white bread with a low gluten content and a thin crust.

In a 9-inch x 13-inch glass baking dish scatter the cubed bread cubes. Set aside.

In a heavy 3-quart saucepan, combine the cream, milk, and 1 1/2 cups granulated sugar. Cut the piece of vanilla bean in half lengthwise, and scrape the seeds into the cream mixture. (Discard the scraped bean pod or add it to granulated or powdered sugar to make vanilla sugar.)

Bring the cream mixture to a simmer over medium-high heat, whisking constantly until the sugar dissolves, then whisking occasionally.Add the chocolate chips and continue cooking until the chocolate is melted, about 2 minutes more, whisking frequently and being sure to scrape the pan bottom clean as you whisk. Remove from heat.

In a large mixing bowl, lightly whisk the eggs until frothy. Very slowly add the chocolate mixture to the eggs, whisking constantly so the eggs don't curdle. Pour this custard mixture over the bread. Let the custard sit until cool enough for you to put your hands in it, about 10 minutes. Once the custard is cool enough, toss the bread cubes with your hands, squeezing the cubes in the liquid to make sure all are well saturated. Cover and refrigerate overnight. About 3 hours before baking the pudding, remove the pan of pudding from the refrigerator, and evenly sprinkle the top with 1/4 cup sugar. Let the pudding sit at room temperature for 45 minutes.

Preheat the oven to 300°F.

Once the pudding has set for 45 minutes (and come to room temperature), seal the baking dish with aluminum foil.

(recipe continued at right)

Ralph Brennan takes as much pleasure in fine tuning restaurants as he does in pleasing guests. Whimsey played at the Red Fish Grill when New Orleans' artist Luis Colmares designed and created the fanciful interior. He made magic from the tabletops to metal ceiling flourishes.

Luis dreamed the restaurant's name while reading "Red Fish, Blue Fish" to his daughters. His head works that way. Wacky, stunning art: see Luis.

Food that sings from New Orleans' heart: see Ralph.

(recipe continued from left)

Bake the pudding until a toothpick inserted in the center comes out almost clean and the pudding looks solidified with no puddles of liquid on the surface, about 2 hours. Once done, it will also start developing a few small, shallow cracks on top and there will be an irresistible smell of chocolate emanating from the oven.

Remove the pudding from the oven and let it sit for 15 minutes at room temperature before serving.

Serve with white and dark chocolate sauce and shaved almond bark.

MONDO
CINNAMON BEIGNETS
WITH HONEYED YOGURT

Chef Susan has always had a soft spot for sweets. It's no surprise that pastry chef Kathryn "Cat" Mann is always busy. Her recipe shows off the beignet's sense of style, as a foundation for creativity.

BEIGNETS
MAKES 1 quart of beignet batter or 24 small beignets

1 cup	water		1 tablespoon	grated orange zest
6 tablespoons	butter		4	eggs
1/8 teaspoon	salt		1 cup	sugar
1 cup	all-purpose flour		1 tablespoon	cinnamon
1 tablespoon	granulated sugar			vegetable oil for frying

HONEY CINNAMON YOGURT
MAKES 1 1/2 cups

1 cup	yogurt		1/2 teaspoon	cinnamon
1/2 cup	honey			

HONEY SAUCE
MAKES 1 cup

1/2 cup	honey		1/2 cup	Pomegranate Molasses

BEIGNET NUTS
MAKES 2 cups

1/2 cup	pistachios		1 1/2 tablespoon	butter
1/2 cup	almonds		to taste	salt
1/2 cup	walnuts		3 tablespoons	sugar
1/2 cup	pecans		1 teaspoon	cinnamon

TO MAKE THE BEIGNETS

In a medium pot, bring water, butter, and salt to a boil. Once boiling, add flour and sugar and reduce heat to medium. Stir quickly with a wooden spoon. When flour and sugar are completely incorporated, the batter should form a ball and pull away from the pot edge.

Remove mixture from heat, add the orange zest and cinnamon, and mix on medium speed until the batter is lukewarm. Add the eggs one at a time, waiting until each is fully incorporated before adding the next.

Fill a large pot no more than halfway with vegetable or canola oil and heat the oil to 350°degrees F. Be very careful with hot oil. Once the oil has reached temperature, using a tablespoon portion,

(recipe continued at left)

(recipe continued from right)
gently drop the doughnuts into the oil. (Once the tops start to puff, flip the doughnuts. Skewers or chop sticks work well for this.) Fry to a medium golden brown, about five minutes, and drain. Toss the beignets in the cinnamon-sugar mixture while they are warm.

TO MAKE THE HONEY SAUCE

Combine honey and Pomegranate Molasses. Pomegranate Molasses can be found at most Middle Eastern Markets and some Asian Markets.

TO MAKE THE CINNAMON HONEY YOGURT

Combine all three ingredients together and whisk until smooth.

Serve as topping over beignets.

TO MAKE THE BEIGNET NUTS

Toast all of the nuts at 325°F for about 5 minutes, until lightly golden

In a medium mixing bowl, melt butter and combine with the nuts. Toss mixture until nuts are well covered. Add salt, sugar, and cinnamon and toss until covered. Spread this nut mixture onto a sheet pan and return to oven for about 1 1/2 minutes to help the butter and sugar mixture adhere to the nuts.

Sprinkle nuts as final topping over beignets and serve.

GRACE BAUER
CLASSIC BEIGNETS

Designer and author Grace Bauer's culinary talents extend to test cooking, not once but as many times as it takes to get it right. Her kitchen assistant, granddaughter Grace Rose, makes certain of that.

Grace authored Los Angeles Classic Desserts, another of the popular series.

Beignets are square fried donuts, no holes, liberally dusted with confectioners' sugar, and served daily all over New Orleans. Some historians believe that the Ursuline Nuns of France brought the beignet recipe to Louisiana in 1727 when they helped to settle the colony.

A beignet may also be used to create savory or sweet canapés and desserts. The crisp exterior embraces fillings such as cheese or seafood stuffing. Simply eliminate the sugar ingredient in the pastry recipe when preparing savories, roll the dough more thinly than directed, cut into rectangles, place a small amount of stuffing on the rectangle and gently fold it over into a square. Pinch the open edges together. Fry as a puffy canapé in 375°F oil. Using the same process for a dessert, keep the sugar in the recipe, and fill the pastry with something sinful, like chocolate or custards.

MAKES 2 dozen 3-inch beignets

1 package, 1/4 ounce	active dry yeast	1	egg, beaten
3/4 cup	warm water	4 to 4 1/4 cups	all-purpose flour
1/4 cup	evaporated milk	1 quart	vegetable oil for frying
1 tablespoon	granulated sugar	1 cup	confectioners' sugar
pinch	salt		

Stir together yeast and 3/4 cup warm water. Let stand for 5 minutes. In a large bowl stir together yeast mixture, evaporated milk, sugar, salt, and egg until blended. Gradually stir in enough flour to make a soft dough. Cover the dough and chill for at least 8 hours.

Place chilled dough on a well-floured surface, and knead 5 or 6 times. Roll dough into a 15-x-15-inch shape, and cut into 3-inch squares.

Into a deep skillet, Dutch oven or fryer, pour oil to depth of 3 or 4 inches and heat to 375°F. Using tongs, place each beignet into the hot oil. Beignets will puff and brown quickly, so do not leave them unattended. Working quickly and not letting them touch, fry several beignets at a time for approximately 1 minute on each side or until golden brown. Using tongs, turn gently to brown each side evenly. Drain well on paper towels and sprinkle hot beignets with confectioners' sugar.

Serve piping hot.

David Spielman

DR. MILBURN CALHOUN
CAFÉ AU LAIT

New Orleans and coffee have been an item for centuries. During the Civil War, ground chicory root stretched scarce coffee beans into a potent brew. New Orleanians became used to the flavor of chicory as a local standard.

A Civil War authority, Dr. Milburn Calhoun, also Pelican's publisher, is specific about many things. Especially when it must be done properly; such as café au lait. Separate pots of hot milk, and coffee with chicory must be poured into the cup at the same time, creating true café au lait.

MAKES 8 cups

4 cups	milk
4 cups	strongly brewed chicory coffee*
to taste	sugar

Brew a double strength pot of chicory coffee. In a medium-sized saucepan, heat the milk until steaming but do not boil.

Pour each liquid into separate coffee pots. Serve by adding them at the same time to individual serving cups.

Sugar may be added individually.

Chicory coffee is available in many markets, or may be ordered online.

CHEF GARY DARLING
BELLINI BABY

A non-alcoholic toast to brunch, a bellini baby is lightly refreshing and sophisticated.

Makes 1 cocktail

1/2 cup   cold peach juice, fresh preferred
1/2 cup   cold club soda or ginger ale
          (replacing traditional Champagne)

Shake the ingredients in shaved ice, and strain into a chilled wine glass.

Marcelle reigns as the Cajun Queen in St. Martinville and lives on Bayou Teche. There she writes cookbooks and columns, and finds time to teach for the John Folse Culinary Institute at Nicholls State University.

Her credits include the Creole Time-Life cookbook, the updated Times Picayune cookbook, and the James Beard Foundation nominated COOKING UP A STORM: Recipes Lost and Found from The Times-Picayune in New Orleans, co-edited with food editor Judy Walker. Marcelle trained with Ella Brennan, matriarch of the Commander's Palace clan and worked with Chef Paul Prudhomme. She collaborated with Emeril Lagasse for his cookbooks, and has made her indelible mark in the food world with charm and talent.

MARCELLE BIENVENU
CREOLE CREAM CHEESE EVANGELINE

Not many recipes evoke longing as Creole cream cheese. More necessity than invention, Creole cream cheese was created due to climate and primitive refrigeration combined with the thrifty Creole waste not want not ethic.

When the milk clabbered the solids separated from the liquid. It was hung in a muslin bag to drain. The solids left in the bag were creamy and tangy and became the focus of the Creole breakfast.

SERVES 6

TO MAKE THE CREOLE CREAM CHEESE

1 gallon   skim milk   1 cup   buttermilk
2   rennet* tablets (or 6-8 drops liquid rennet)

Dissolve rennet tablets in 1/2 cup of warm, not hot, water.

Using a large glass or stainless steel bowl (no aluminum, please, it will react negatively), combine milk, buttermilk, and rennet. Cover with plastic wrap.

Stand at room temperature for 24-36 hours until mixture separates into whey and curds. The clear liquid on the top is the whey. The heavier, fluffy solid curds sink to the bottom.

Line a colander with 2 layers of cheesecloth, allowing 2 inches to drape over the edges of the colander to avoid slipping when straining out the whey. Place colander over a large bowl and slowly pour off the whey liquid and discard, reserving the curds left in the cheesecloth. Place the curds in a container. Cover and refrigerate 48 hours.

Add fresh fruit, sprinkle with sugar and cinnamon, and enjoy.

TO MAKE THE EVANGELINE

2 cups   heavy cream   2 cups   fruit cut in bite-size pieces
4 ounces   Creole cream cheese   3 tablespoons   orange juice
3 tablespoons   sugar

Place cream, Creole cream cheese and sugar in a stainless steel bowl and whisk until thoroughly blended. Cover and refrigerate until serving time.

Select seasonal fruit such as seedless grapes, apples, fresh berries, pears, and bananas. Cut fruit in bite-size pieces into a glass or stainless steel bowl and toss with 3 tablespoons orange juice to prevent darkening. Refrigerate until time to serve.

To serve, ladle the Creole cream cheese mixture into the bottom of ice cream or parfait glasses. Spoon fruit over and top with an additional tablespoon of the cheese mixture. Garnish with a sprig of fresh mint.

NOTE: A fast substitute, not quite the same thing, but very close is to blend 2 ounces sour cream and 2 ounces cream cheese.

Rennet tablets are available at most pharmacies.

CHEF SUSAN SPICER
Lemon Ricotta Crepes
with Ricotta Filling and Lemon Compote

MAKES 16 crepes

1 cup	milk	1/4 cup	confectioners' sugar
2 tablespoons	granulated sugar	1/8 teaspoon	salt
2 tablespoons	butter, plus more for frying	1 teaspoon	orange zest
3	eggs	1 teaspoon	lemon zest
3/4 cup	flour, sifted		

Heat the milk and granulated sugar in a small saucepan over medium-high heat until the milk just begins to bubble. Remove it from the heat and stir in the butter. Place in a blender and slowly add the eggs, flour, confectioners' sugar, and salt. Blend until thoroughly combined, then pulse in the zests. Let the batter rest about 15 minutes to release any air bubbles.

Melt 1 teaspoon of butter in an 8-inch nonstick pan over medium heat. Pour 2 tablespoons of batter into the pan. Tilt and swirl the pan until the batter covers the bottom completely. Keep rolling the batter toward the outer rim so that the edges do not get too thin. When the edges begin to turn golden, flip the crepe with a plastic spatula and cook approximately 30 seconds on the other side. Slide the crepe out of the pan onto the cooling rack or baking sheet. Repeat with the remaining batter.

RICOTTA CHEESE FILLING

1 cup	Ricotta cheese	1 teaspoon	pure vanilla extract
1/2 cup	mascarpone	2 tablespoons	orange juice
2 tablespoons	sugar		

Combine all the ingredients in a food processor, or a mixer with the paddle attachment, and process until smooth and slightly creamy. Taste and adjust to preference.

LEMON COMPOTE

2	lemons, peel and all, sliced in rings to 1/16 inch thick	1 1/2 cups	orange juice
		1/4 cup	lemon juice
1/2	vanilla bean, split and scraped	1/2 cup	sugar

Combine all items in a saucepan and simmer over medium-low heat, stirring occasionally, until the lemon peels become completely translucent and the liquid is thick and syrupy. Remove from heat and remove vanilla bean.

Bayona is another good reason New Orleans attracts food lovers from around the world. Chef Susan Spicer earned her culinary chops as an apprentice in New Orleans. Forming a partnership with Regina Keever, they opened Bayona in a beautiful, 200-year-old cottage in the French Quarter. With solid support from local diners and critics, Bayona soon earned national attention, accolades, awards, and has been featured in numerous publications. A cool patio nestles behind restaurant on Dauphine Street, which carried the name Camino de Bayona during New Orleans' Spanish colonial period.

Susan's take on international cuisine is found in many of her favorite recipes, and her style is pure serendipity, with Big Easy flavor. Among her prestigious professional honors is her selection by the James Beard Foundation in 1993 as Best Chef, Southeast. In 2010, she was inducted into the James Beard Foundation's Who's Who of Food and Beverage in America.

Susan's cookbook, Crescent City Cooking: Unforgettable Recipes from Susan Spicer's New Orleans, *is an exciting, must-have addition to any kitchen bookshelf.*

Her latest venture is MONDO, a popular casual, family style restaurant in the Lakeview neighborhood.

Roux

Roux thickens sauces, gravies, and stocks but also adds an unmistakable undertone of taste. It is a mixture of flour and fat that is slowly cooked before adding to liquid. The fat may be butter, clarified butter, bacon fat, vegetable, or olive oil. The proportions tend to be a matter of personal preference. The basis is one-to-one but slightly more flour may be added if the roux seems too thin. Taste will vary based on color. A blond roux should take five to 10 minutes, a medium roux 15 to 20 minutes, and the dark roux as much as an hour, at a very low flame. Once a roux has been started, it must be constantly attended.

Using a heavy bottomed skillet or Dutch oven over medium heat, add the oil and warm. Begin stirring in the flour gradually. Lower the heat to a summer and continue stirring until the color is reached.

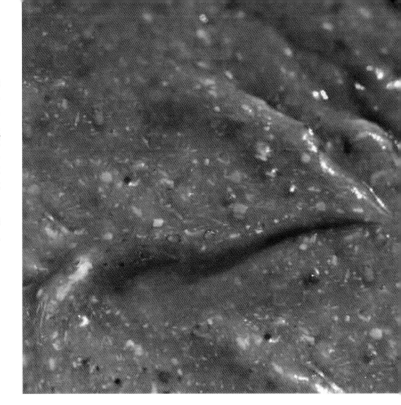

Remoulade Sauce

MAKES about 1 cup

1 tablespoon	lemon juice
1/2 cup	olive oil
1/4 cup	Creole whole-grain mustard
1 tablespoon	prepared horseradish
1/2 teaspoon	Louisiana hot sauce
1/4 cup	ketchup
	pepper, to taste
	cayenne pepper, to taste

Without the salt and peppers, pulse all ingredients in the bowl of a food processor or blender. Once well combined, season to taste. Cover and store in the refrigerator.

Fresh Bouquet Garni

Bouquet garni is the French term for a bundle of fresh herbs tied together and tossed into the pot. It is then removed so the seasonings do not remain in the dish.

Any appropriate herbs may be combined to make a bouquet garni. Tie the sprigs together with cooking twine and drop them in the pot. Or, enclose herbs or dry seasonings in a 7-inch square of cheesecloth; draw the four corners together at the top and tie into a little pouch. Use a tea ball if the quantity is small enough. When the cooking is completed, fish the herbs out with a slotted spoon and discard.

CHOCOLATE SAUCE

1 cup	heavy cream
1/2 cup	granulated sugar
3/4 cup	semi-sweet chocolate chips
1 tablespoon	unsalted butter

In a heavy 1-quart saucepan, combine the cream and sugar. Bring the mixture to a simmer over medium-high heat, whisking until the sugar is dissolved. Reduce the heat to low and gradually add the chocolate chips, whisking until each addition is completely melted into the cream before adding more. Add the butter and continue cooking, whisking constantly, until the butter is incorporated into the sauce. Remove from the heat.

WHITE CHOCOLATE SAUCE

10 ounces (2 1/2 cups)	white chocolate chips
1 1/2 cups	heavy cream
3 tablespoons	unsalted butter
1 tablespoon	granulated sugar

Place the white-chocolate chips in a medium-size mixing bowl and set aside. In a heavy 2-quart saucepan, combine the cream, butter and sugar. Bring the mixture to a boil over medium-high heat, whisking constantly. Remove from heat and pour the cream mixture over the reserved chips, whisking until the mixture is smooth.

ALMOND BARK

Almond Bark can be purchased already made, but that would be cheating.

1/2 cup	chopped almonds
4 cups (24-ounces)	fine-quality bittersweet chocolate chips
3 cups (16 1/2-ounces)	fine-quality white chocolate chips

Preheat the oven to 325°F.

Roast the almonds in a small baking pan until light golden, about 5 minutes, stirring once or twice. Watch them carefully so they don't over-brown.

Line a rimmed baking sheet, about 17 by 12 inches by 1 inch, with parchment paper. Set aside.

Melt the bittersweet chocolate chips in the top of a double boiler over hot (not simmering) water, stirring until smooth. Remove the top of the pan from over the hot water when the chips are about half-way melted to stir thoroughly.

Once the chocolate is smooth, remove it from heat and promptly pour it onto the baking sheet, spreading it in a thin, even layer with an icing spatula.

Refrigerate, uncovered, until firm, about 15 minutes.

While the dark chocolate is chilling, melt the white chocolate chips as you did the dark ones. Take extra care to heat the white chocolate over very low heat, since white chocolate scorches more easily than dark chocolate. Also, wash and dry the icing spatula.

Once the white chocolate is melted and the dark chocolate is firm, remove the dark chocolate from the refrigerator.

Immediately spread the white chocolate evenly over the dark chocolate with the icing spatula, working quickly so the warmth of the white chocolate barely has time to melt the dark chocolate. (Don't worry if it melts a little. It will give the white chocolate a pretty marbled look.)

Promptly sprinkle the almonds over the white chocolate, breaking them into coarse crumbs as you go, and gently pressing them into the chocolate to make sure they stick. Refrigerate the candy, uncovered, until just firm. After 30 to 40 minutes the candy should be firm enough to break into rough 2-inch pieces of "bark." Don't refrigerate until very firm before breaking into bark or the chocolate will be more difficult to break up.

Serving Suggestion: Use immediately or keep refrigerated, separated by sheets of wax paper, in airtight containers. The candy will keep at least one week.

HOLLANDAISE SAUCE
Makes 1 1/2 Cups

Hollandaise can be tricky and it waits for no one. If the sauce or the butter cool too much as you whisk, the butter will begin to harden and thicken. If so, add a few drops of warm water. If the sauce looks as if it is about to separate, immediately whisk in a few tablespoons of cold water.

You can save some time by making hollandaise in a blender. Process for about 1 minute the egg yolks and the lemon juice, then, with the machine running, gradually add the warm to hot clarified butter. The sauce should thicken by the time all the butter is incorporated, about 1 1/2 minutes. Season to taste and serve it immediately.

1 1/2 cups (3 sticks)	cold unsalted butter (clarified)
6	large egg yolks
2 tablespoons	white wine
1 tablespoon	water
	kosher salt and cayenne pepper to taste
	Hot sauce to taste if desired

In a small saucepan over low heat, melt butter. Using a spoon skim away white foam (milk solids) to make clarified butter. Cool to warm.

Whisk yolks, wine, and 1 tablespoon water in a bowl until light and frothy. Place the top of the double boiler or the bowl over barely simmering water and continue to whisk until eggs are thickened, about 4 minutes, being careful not to let the eggs get too hot. Remove the pan or bowl from over the water and whisk to slightly cool mixture. Slowly add warm clarified butter, whisking constantly. Whisk in salt and cayenne pepper and season with hot sauce. If sauce is too thick whisk in a few drops of warm water.

TO MAKE ORANGE HOLLANDAISE

To make orange hollandaise add 1 to 3 teaspoons lemon juice as well as 2 teaspoons freshly grated orange zest to the sauce when you add the salt.

TO MAKE BACON HORSERADISH HOLLANDAISE

Add 3 tablespoons crumbled cooked bacon and 2 teaspoons prepared horseradish to the sauce when you add the salt and pepper.

CANDIED PECANS
MAKES 2 cups

Preheat oven to 250°F.

2 cups	pecan halves or pieces
1 tablespoon	dark brown sugar
1/2 teaspoon	cinnamon or nutmeg, optional
	Pinch salt

Cover a baking sheet with baking parchment. Melt the butter in skillet then add the sugar, cinnamon, and salt. Stir until all of the sugar has dissolved. Add the pecans, tossing gently in the sugar-butter mixture until evenly coated. Remove the pecans with a slotted spoon. Spread pecans evenly on a parchment covered or greased baking sheet and place in the oven for 30 to 45 minutes, until golden brown and aromatic. Remove from oven and cool. They may be kept in a covered container for up to a week.

TOASTED PECANS
MAKES 2 cups

Preheat oven to 250°F.

2 cups	pecans

Cover a baking sheet with baking parchment. Spread pecans evenly on a baking sheet and place in the oven for 30 to 45 minutes. Watch carefully until golden brown and aromatic. Remove from oven and cool. They may be kept in a covered container for up to a week or frozen in a zip lock bag for up to 3 months.

These hands belong to a sister, wife, mother, grandmother, great-grandmother, neighbor, friend, and New Orleans icon. They are the hands of Leah Chase. Not only have they cuddled 23 great-grandchildren, they've stirred thousands of pots of gumbo. The Reverend Doctor Martin Luther King, Jr. had a bowlful. So have several U.S. Presidents, Thurgood Marshall, James Baldwin, Count Basie, Sarah Vaughn, Lena Horne, Duke Ellington, and Ray Charles. Tomorrow, she'll be happy to feed you. "I still cook," she says. And the hands don't lie.

INDEX

ACKNOWLEDGEMENTS

Of all the people who made this book possible, the chefs and restaurateurs who make New Orleans a great food town are the most important. They each have dedicated staff to back them up, wizards all, including Julie Brignac, Wesley Noble Janssen, Christina Marciante, Lovey Wakefield and Bonnie Warren.

Grace Bauer and Erin Hicks Miller, dear friends and authors for the *Classic Series* in other cities, were here with support when it counted. Linda Ellerbee gave her laughter and wry advice. Literary agent Maura Kye-Casella is my rock.

Art director Michael Lauve managed to keep his sense of humor. Once again, the terrific staff at Pelican Publishing made this new *Classic Series* addition a joy. Marci Schramm and her colleagues at the French Quarter Festival produce New Orleans greatest entertainers: food, music and leisure to enjoy them. Thank you all for your contributions.

A legion of photographers, magnificent creative people, offered brilliant shots and insight. Paul Rico and Rolfe Tessem help me see the light. William Jones Miller and Mary Lou Uttermohlen contributed greatly. Margo Landen and David Spielman also provided stunning images.

It takes many large and small hands to make a book. Special kudos to Barry Garner, Eloisa Zepeda and Hartley Casbon for their assistance. Neglected friends and family never fail to encourage and forgive me. I adore you all.

As always, I own any omissions or errors. I enjoy hearing from you. As an experiment, Facebook foodies tried recipes, then weighed in with their opinions. That was such fun.

My appreciation and love go to Billy, my husband, who makes it all happen.

Mary Lou Uttermohlen